COPS
&
DOUGHNUTS

COPS
&
DOUGHNUTS

HOW A POLICE DEPARTMENT
SAVED A HISTORIC BAKERY AND
PUT A SMALL TOWN ON THE MAP

AS TOLD BY THE COP OWNERS
TO ANNE STANTON

MISSION POINT PRESS

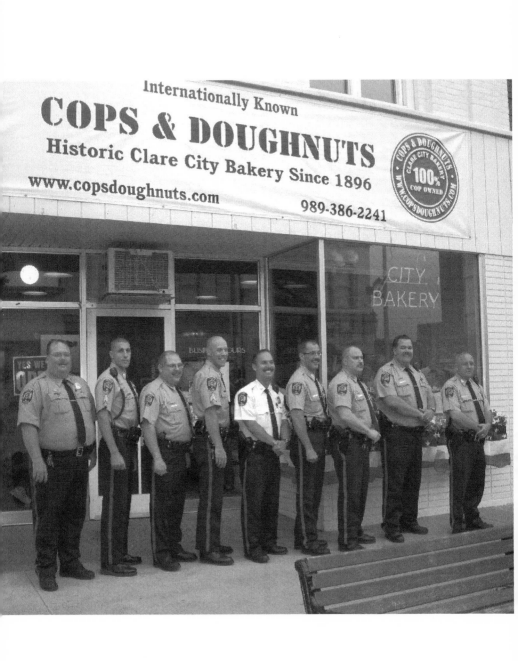

The nine Clare City cops who launched the bakery into the national stratosphere: Alan "Bubba" White, David "Grasshopper" Saad, John "Beaver" Pedjac, Richard "Junior" Ward, Dwayne "Midge" Miedzianowski, Brian "Dogman" Gregory, Greg "Bulldog" Kolhoff, Greg "Ryno" Rynearson, and Jeremy "Squirt" McGraw.

The nine cop owners, pictured from top left
and clockwise:

Alan "Bubba" White
Dwayne "Midge" Miedzianowski
Jeremy "Squirt" McGraw
Richard "Junior" Ward
Greg "Bulldog" Kolhoff
Greg "Ryno" Rynearson
John "Beaver" Pedjac
Brian "Dogman" Gregory
David "Grasshopper" Saad (center photo)

To connect with the authors or to order this book in bulk, please
email info.copsdoughnuts@gmail.com.

To order doughnuts, please visit www.copsdoughnuts.com.

Published by Mission Point Press
2554 Chandler Rd.
Traverse City, MI 49696
(231) 421-9513
www.MissionPointPress.com

ISBN: 978-1-958363-19-5
Library of Congress Control Number:

Printed in the United States of America

We dedicate this book to the men and women of law enforcement.

"Blessed are the peacemakers, for they will be called children of God." (Matthew 5:9)

CONTENTS

FOREWORD

The Cops & Doughnuts story is a unique blend of extraordinary entrepreneurship, brilliant business acumen, marketing genius, ingenuity, hard work, courage, risk-taking, humor, first-class customer service, dedication, compassion, and sometimes simple dumb luck. It is a story that embodies the human spirit and is testimony to what can be accomplished even in times of uncertainty and in the face of challenge and adversity. A true success story but with bumps and bruises from being knocked down, then getting back up, shaking oneself off, learning from mistakes and being better for them.

This book is an excellent primer for any individual or group with ambitions of starting a business and serves as a great example of a start-up business succeeding even during a time of economic hardship. It is replete with vignettes of great marketing practices, the intelligent use of social media and how the application of both contributed immensely to the success of this nationally famous business. The moxie of nine full-time cops to step up and buy the historic downtown bakery despite having near-zero business experience is a model for anyone whose timidity and indecision are preventing them from pursuing their own dreams of business ownership.

The primary motivation for the nine police officers in buying the bakery was to help curb the trend of closing businesses in the downtown district of their small community—to ensure that their hometown of Clare, Michigan, remained a great place to live, work, and raise a family. Their immense success not only bolstered the existing downtown businesses but added an element of renewed excitement in the downtown that eventually resulted in filling vacant storefronts with new businesses, many of them headed by local first-time business owners just like the police officers who own Cops & Doughnuts. This story proves once again that success breeds success.

There are a number of examples in the book that aptly demonstrate the commitment, dedication, and love these police officers have for their community. They are justly considered hometown heroes who care deeply about the people who call Clare home, and they have a well-earned reputation for stepping up to help when needed.

The owners of Cops & Doughnuts are real cops and are real people. "Ryno" and "Bubba" are the company's president and vice president, respectively. You will find one or both of them at the bakery in Clare every Monday–Friday and oftentimes on Saturday and Sunday. If you have interest in their amazing story, I encourage you to read the book. And then come visit the bakery in Clare, Michigan. I know they'll be happy to have a photo taken with you and willingly share the Cops & Doughnuts story with you personally.

Ken Hibl
Former Clare City Manager & Colonel (Ret.), US Army

INTRODUCTION

The Cops & Doughnuts bakery first opened its doors in Clare, a tiny Michigan town, in the early morning of July 1, 2009. The fragrance of fresh-fried doughnuts wafted out into the warm air, permeating the downtown with a homey, nostalgic feeling.

No one could have guessed at the chaos erupting within.

Just hours before, John Pedjac, a Clare city cop, was frying up doughnuts—or at least attempting to. John, who goes by the nickname of Beaver, was under pressure to make doughnuts for the big opening but had already burned or under-cooked hundreds of them.

"There's no other way to learn how to make good ones than making bad ones," said Beaver, who was learning Doughnut Flipping 101 at age 41. "If you leave the doughnut in too long—it can be just a matter of ten seconds too long—you'll get a hard-as-rock doughnut. If you take it out too fast, it's raw dough inside. You have to look at the color and watch when it changes—when it darkens up—and memorize that color. Then you flip two dozen of 'em real quick."

Beaver felt overwhelmed but wouldn't have it any other way.

"I started as a paramedic and got involved in law enforcement, and I live for the pressure. When the crap hits the fan is when the cream rises to the top," he said, mixing metaphors as skillfully as he does doughnut dough.

After a grueling week of flipping doughnuts, John "Beaver" Pedjac sips to early success.

With him was Greg "Bulldog" Kolhoff, another Clare cop with a muscular, don't-mess-with-me build as his nickname would suggest. They were squeezed into a cramped kitchen, side by side with Toni Jablonski, the bakery's co-owner who had agreed to assist for a week. She relented to stay on for another out of pity for the cops and new bakery workers alike. Overseeing it all was Wayne Wekwert, the just-hired manager whose true talent was processing venison for area hunters. And nervously awaiting the doors to open for the first time was a small crew of teenagers who had never worked a cash register before.

Bakery manager Wayne Wekwert, after working all night, runs on pure adrenaline on opening day.

Just two months before, neither Beaver nor Bulldog would have imagined in their wildest dreams they'd be frying dough-nuts in a dreary, hot and steamy kitchen with no air condition-ing. They were two of the nine cop owners who decided to buy the bakery on a whim when the Clare City Bakery announced in May that it was closing its doors after a 113-year run.

It was a rescue of sorts. The cops had already seen ten oth-er businesses shutter their doors in Clare, a friendly town of 3,100, known as the "gateway" to northern Michigan's resort towns of big trees and sparkling blue lakes. They feared the downtown would slowly fade away as the Internet and big-box stores relentlessly siphoned off business.

COPS & DOUGHNUTS

Former owner Toni Jablonski with employees Ashley Drury (left) and Ashley Thomas.

Some of the cops had grown up in Clare, while others moved to the closely knit community more recently. None of them wanted to bear witness to still another retail casualty of the 2008 recession, which left the city with a 19 percent unemployment rate. So, the cops pooled enough money to buy the bakery and revitalize the downtown. Beaver, who bears an uncanny resemblance to Beaver of *Leave It to Beaver* fame, said the Clare cops have a saying, "When everyone does good, everyone does good." What he meant was full employment means a safer, happier community.

And to be blunt, the nine cops also invested in the bakery out of self-interest; they had hopes of making some extra dough to supplement their modest salaries.

Their first task was figuring out how to tell their story to the media. They decided on just being themselves: earnest, goofy and good-hearted. Instead of running away from a negative, arguably offensive stereotype of cops hanging out at a doughnut shop, they decided to go big in every possible way, from doughnut names—Felony Fritter and The Squealer—to the bakery's badge-shaped sign with a pink-frosted doughnut to the bakery bathrooms, painted with jail bars and a chained padlock. And embedded in the story line was their honest-to-goodness attempt to revive their beloved town.

They had a hunch that their story, just like a dozen warm doughnuts, would be too good to resist. So, before opening day, they huddled together and decided they would get the media to come to their beloved town of Clare.

"We were going to make the news come to *us* to do an interview," declared Greg "Ryno" Rynearson when the cops gathered one evening to talk policy. "They bring their cameras here to Clare. They help *us*. They help *us* save the community."

In those dizzying first ten days, the cops would be showcased on *Good Morning America, Fox & Friends,* CNN, and profiled in dozens of worldwide newspapers. Over the course of a decade, the bakery would thrive, go nearly bankrupt in a failed attempt to franchise, and then regroup and financially recover.

Today, the bakery is a $3.4 million enterprise and includes the Clare bakery "headquarters," three additional "precincts" or bakeries, nine "substations" across Michigan, and an active website that sells merchandise and ships doughnuts across the country. Their Facebook page has more than 66,000 followers. The Clare bakery site alone brings in $35,000 over a single summer weekend. That compares to the original bakery, which grossed $89,000 in the twelve months prior to the cops taking over.

Bubba and Greg "Ryno" Rynearson—two cops with personalities as big as their body types—head the bakery, Ryno as president and Bubba as second-in-command. Both retired from the Clare police force and now work full-time managing and marketing the statewide enterprise. But all nine cops were responsible for buying the bakery and launching it into a national phenomenon.

The cops' dream of "giving back" to the town came true. Visit Clare today, and you'll see only a few vacant storefronts in the downtown. The cop owners have gone even a step further. Using their bakery profits, the nine cop owners have helped countless nonprofits and people down on their luck.

This is their story.

COPS
&
DOUGHNUTS

A photo of the bakery in 1926.

Chapter 1

OPENING A BAKERY AND FEELING FRIED

On the morning of May 29, 2009, the last Friday in May, Greg "Ryno" Rynearson, a Clare city cop, was enjoying a farmer's omelet for breakfast at Herrick House, an elegant restaurant in the small town of Clare.

A local businessman sat down and ordered coffee and spilled the latest news: after 113 years, the Clare City Bakery was closing. Ryno, a math whiz (unbeknownst to his high school teachers as he rarely showed up for class), did a quick calculation—the bakery opened in 1896, thirty years after the Civil War ended! No way, he thought, would he let it close on his watch.

Ryno drove to the City of Clare Police Department and announced the news to John "Beaver" Pedjac, who worked the desk, and Alan White, his patrol partner and longtime colleague

The bakery in 2009, just before Cops & Doughnuts took ownership.

who went by Bubba. They had both attended Clare public schools together, Ryno barely graduating with a 1.7 GPA. As he would say, it was a "poor fit." But he soon proved himself at the police academy, graduating at the top of the class with a 4.0. Bubba and Ryno were often patrol mates—they both joined the Clare Police force in 1982. (Bubba took off two years from the force to work as a cop in Alaska.)

Now Ryno and Bubba were forty-six and ready for a new challenge. They had been talking for a few months about buying the bakery and would often joke that "wouldn't it be something if a couple of old cops bought the bakery"—not that they were exactly old. Some years back, it had closed but sold right away, and they'd given up on the idea. But they could see the new-ish owner was struggling and it looked like the bakery wouldn't make it. They had another bite at the doughnut, so to speak.

"Here's a chance for us to buy it," Bubba told Ryno at lunch.

And by "us," he meant the entire Clare Police Department.

The three officers decided to explore the idea. Ryno left the table to call Tom Kunse, who was married to Janet, a co-owner of the bakery along with her mom, Toni Jablonski.

"Are you really closing?" Ryno asked.

"Yep."

"Would you lease it to us with an option to buy?"

"Sure, we would."

"Can you give me a lease price right now?"

"Yep, just a second."

Ryno heard him punching on the calculator.

"A thousand dollars a month."

"How about the purchase price if we paid your debt right off?"

2

More calculator punching.

"You could buy it for $160,000 with all the equipment, all the recipes, everything."

Ryno went back to Bubba and Beaver and they did a back-of-the-pizza-box calculation. If all nine cops pitched in $1,500 each, they'd have $13,500—enough to buy product and make payroll. Ryno was aware that a few officers with young families couldn't afford it, so he threw in an option to deposit $400 now and make $100 payments for eleven months.

Word spread in the cop shop, and all were in. But they quickly learned that they had to get the bakery open by July 1—four weeks away!

NINE COPS PULL TOGETHER

The July 1 date was beyond realistic, but there were two reasons for the insanity. First, bakery co-owner Toni Jablonski decided she was going to close the bakery on July 1 and take a vacation soon afterward. The cops would need her to stay on for at least a week to show the new workers the ropes. Secondly, the bakery was barely up to code.

"If the bakery closed and we tried to reopen six months later, we'd have to put in hundreds of thousands of dollars to bring it up to code," Bubba said. "But if the bakery continued operating until July 1, everything was grandfathered in. So, we were under a time crunch."

The bakery was dated, to say the least—nothing had been done to it after years of razor-thin profits. The cop owners were intent on giving the bakery a fresh face before opening day.

"We wanted to paint. Old wallpaper had to come down. We wanted people to come in and see it fresh," Bubba said.

COPS & DOUGHNUTS

Top: Cop owner Dwayne "Midge" Miedzianowski stepping up to clean a light. Middle: Bubba after an exhausting day of painting. Bottom: Cop owner Jeremy "Squirt" McGraw stops in to admire progress of his fellow officers.

"When you came in before, it wasn't depressing, but there was no energy there. We just wanted to change that. It was all-hands-on-deck. If you weren't on duty, you were working and painting and scrubbing, and all our wives and girlfriends were down here, too. My wife was here every night after work. It was really hectic. This whole time, we had no idea if it was going to be a success."

Officer Brian "Dogman" Gregory remembers the long hours they put in but also how much fun they had.

"We were all working together trying to make that old building presentable. But it was such a time crunch, it was kind of pressure packed."

Ryno's son pitched in not only with creating a new website, but also making a CD with cop songs, Bubba said.

"He had them all. 'I Fight Authority and Authority Always Wins,' 'Indiana Wants Me' . . . We played it on a continuous loop before we knew it was illegal,"

4

Bubba said of the cops' first incident of accidentally breaking the law.

On June 7, the nine cops gathered at the bakery, which was closed on Sundays. They were there to check out the space and to agree on a name. One cop suggested "9-1-1 Doughnuts." A lot of them liked "The Cop Shop." They were just about to vote, when a young voice floated above the chatter.

"Hey Dad, I don't like the name Cop Shop."

All eyes turned on Brendan, the young son of Dogman (so named because he was the department's expert dog trainer). Brendan had been lying on the floor playing a computer game, and no one thought he was listening.

"All the kids play cops and robbers," he said. "Why don't you call it cops and doughnuts?"

The room exploded with chatter and the nine cops immediately agreed it was a terrific name.

That night Ryno went home to see if the web domain www.copsanddonuts.com was available. It was already taken by a franchise that went out of business. He tried again with www.copsdoughnuts.com.

And it was available. A (doughnut) hole in one! So, that's how the bakery name ended up with the proper spelling of "doughnuts." Ryno would later explain that Clare cops just happened to be sticklers for proper spelling.

The cops began brainstorming ideas for T-shirts, coffee cups and hoodies: "You Have the Right to Remain Glazed"; "Handcuffs and Cream Puffs"; "Cereal Killer" and "D.W.I. — Doughnuts Were Involved." Ryno's son, Lance, created the bakery's website, which sold merchandise through Zebra Press. Meanwhile, Bubba and his wife, Nettie, worked Sundays finding and

COPS & DOUGHNUTS

CopsDoughnuts.com

Clare Michigan

The Cops & Doughnuts logo that pairs a police badge with a delicate white frosting and sprinkles.

ordering merchandise to sell in the bakery. The bakery's original official logo looked like a police badge—"100% Cop Owned." But after a month, Ryno showed that sales were stronger when merchandise was adorned with a more whimsical-looking logo that Beaver had come up with: a frosted doughnut wrapped around a police badge.

"That's what was getting ordered 80 percent of the time. We have to take our orders from the customers," Ryno told the officers, who were unused to taking orders from anyone.

With the opening two weeks away, the to-do list was piling up, and Ryno took two weeks off to get the supplies together, pull a permit from the health department, open a bank account, and do the paperwork for the LLC. The bookkeeper, the accountant, and an attorney agreed to give the bakery a little sugar and work for free.

"The whole community came together," Ryno said. "We were the guys who were doing it, but everybody stepped up."

Ryno advanced the money whenever they were short. Beaver suggested his brother-in-law step in as head baker since he had a little experience in a doughnut shop in Alpena, Michigan. Beaver and Greg "Bulldog" Kolhoff immediately started training with co-owner Toni Jablonski.

The counter staff with opening-day smiles.

Bubba, a school officer, handpicked his favorite 15- and 16-year-olds to man the cash register and bag the doughnuts, bread and merchandise.

The nine cops met together on June 14 for the last time before the bakery opening two weeks away, bringing their wives and checkbooks to the Big Boy restaurant. There was a lot to talk about. First off, some were upset with Ryno for buying 72 mugs with the Cops & Doughnuts logo.

"What are you doing buying so many?" Bubba griped. "That's six dozen mugs. Do you know how long it's going to take to go through those?"

As it turned out: a single weekend.

Bubba thought it would take forever to sell the bakery's first 72 mugs. Within two days, they were gone.

ALL EYES ON CLARE

The first day opened with a bang.

Beaver, Bulldog, Toni and Wayne started frying doughnuts at midnight—enough doughnuts, they thought, to last the entire next day.

Dogman greets Dr. Elmer Surlow, the town's medical examiner and the bakery's very first customer.

They finished up around 3 a.m. and went home for a couple of hours to sleep before returning again at 6 a.m. But by 11 a.m., the bakery was running out of raised doughnuts, and Beaver had to act quickly.

"We decided to make cake doughnuts. That was the fastest

thing we could throw out. It only takes a half hour. It takes hours for the raised ones."

The nine cops all pitched in, splitting time between their regular jobs and the bakery that week. Jeremy "Squirt" McGraw's thing was dishes. He'd come in and do dishes for hours and hours. Bubba fielded media calls and Ryno fought fires inside the bakery.

"We did everything that first week," Ryno said. "I would come down, still in uniform, and help out when I got out of work. We were running around like crazy; we didn't know what we were doing. We were trying to help with everything. We were so busy behind the counter that our wives and kids had to come in and help."

Despite the pressure, the cops chatted with the customers, signing autographs on their doughnut bags, doughnut boxes, hoodies, cups and shirts. Beaver thought to himself: "You've gotta be kidding me. I'm a copper, and you want my signature?"

A reporter with the *Mount Pleasant Morning Sun*, Sue Fields, stopped by on opening day to interview Bubba and Ryno. TV 5 showed up later in the day, right around the time when Ryno delivered a bag of doughnuts and Cops & Doughnuts shirts to band members of the band Night Shift performing in the park. The reporter told them he planned on uploading the local segment to CNN.

All-hands-on-dough! Pictured here are Jordan and Rachael, Beaver's kids.

"I'm thinking, 'Wow, CNN!'" Ryno said. "But CNN did not play it. They said there's no story here."

Their first setback.

By Thursday morning, CNN's rejection was a distant memory. The nine cops found themselves on the front page of the *Morning Sun*. Lucky for them, Matt Small, then an Associated Press reporter in the Washington, D.C. bureau, had noticed the article on the wire and decided to give them a call. He was skeptical. Was it a joke? Cops making fun of themselves? Seriously? He asked to talk to a cop.

"Speaking," Bubba said.

"I just saw this story on Cops & Doughnuts. Is it for real? I mean, this can't be a real story," he said.

"Of course, it's real," Bubba said. "But if you don't believe me, you can call the editor Rick Mills at the *Morning Sun* and ask him."

Small hung up and dialed the paper.

"Is it for real?"

"Oh, yeah," said Mills. "I know those guys. It's for real."

Small called Bubba again and scheduled an interview later in the day. By the time they connected, Bubba was in his patrol car and needed a quiet place to talk. He drove to the far end of the Clare cemetery, where no one would see him except a possible mourner. Over the course of forty-five minutes, he spilled the story.

"Alan," the reporter said to him (because reporters aren't comfortable calling a stranger Bubba), "I don't know whether to laugh or to cry. On the one hand, it's a very touching story. You've got the little town in the middle of the Rust Belt that has got all these closed storefronts and the little dough-nut shop that just couldn't make it anymore. And who comes along but a bunch of civic-minded cops. So, like I said, very touching, but on the other hand, it's a really *funny* story. I don't think you guys have any idea what's about to happen to you. This is going to hit the AP [Associated Press] wire and every single place on the planet will read about you except maybe Antarctica."

Small was right. On Friday morning, the story of Cops & Doughnuts landed in thousands of newspapers like a tsunami. One reporter after another called the bakery, asking for an in-terview and wrote stories sprinkled with puns: "Michigan cops protect and serve" . . . "Cops & Doughnuts: An arresting suc-cess." They couldn't resist listing the names of the specialty doughnuts: Felony Fritters, Nightsticks, and The Squealer.

While Bubba talked on the phone with Ron Jolly on WTCM-AM in Traverse City, ninety minutes north, Ryno was literally halfway down the block talking to another reporter. Entrepre-neurs rang the bakery about franchise opportunities. Tempers began to fray and the noise level inside the bakery rose to a dull roar. It was hard to hear customers. Bubba was tired and grumpy.

"Cops & Doughnuts," he yelled into the phone.

"Hi, this is Dawn Foods down in Jackson."

Bubba recognized the name. It was the place where the bakery bought its flour, sugar, and other supplies.

"I understand that the bakery changed hands. Are you one of the owners?"

"Yes!" yelled Bubba.

COPS & DOUGHNUTS

"Well, I want to come up there and show you ways to get more customers to come into the bakery."

"That ain't the problem!" Bubba yelled. "Get up here and help!"

And he did. Within three days, the technician arrived with dozens of bags of flour and sugar and stayed for several days to train the cops on the finer points of making doughnuts.

On Friday morning the word was clearly out, and people lined up down the block to get in as soon as the bakery's doors opened. Many had driven from all over the state, including the National Cherry Festival in Traverse City, where they heard about the bakery from a live interview on WTCM-AM, northern Michigan's largest AM station.

Ironically, the Clare cops had no time to do what cops allegedly do. Eat doughnuts and sip coffee.

Dogman and Ryno take out time for a heartfelt hug.

People were excited. Cops happily signed autographs, a bit dazzled by the attention, and it felt like a party.

But back in the hot kitchen, things had grown tense. Take bakery manager Wayne Wekwert, who had never managed an operation of this magnitude. He was Beaver's former brother-in-law at the time and didn't appreciate that all nine cops, all with alpha personalities, wanted to be the boss and kept confronting him with problems.

"That's what we had to nip in the bud. We decided if we've got a problem, it can only go to Bubba or Dogman [the official spokesman], or Bulldog," Beaver said. "Wayne couldn't have all nine of us going to him every day. You just can't have nine bosses, all of us wanting everything to be perfect. That was the biggest thing, almost immediately."

An even bigger problem: they were quickly running out of doughnut mix. Bubba made calls to area bakeries, begging

"You just can't have nine bosses, all of us wanting everything to be perfect."

for help. A Mount Pleasant bakery had some bags they could spare and so did the Amish bakery outside of town.

"We were going through so much product we couldn't keep up at all," Bubba said. "There's a Gordon Food Service in Mount Pleasant. My wife and I screamed down there in my truck, just started hauling stuff off the shelves like muffins and stuff, and I'm in the back seat, taking the wrappers off everything. We threw that stuff on trays just to have something to sell."

The bakery stayed open all weekend. Dogman was mopping up as the exhausted workers were packing it in. The phone rang at 5:45 p.m. Bubba picked up.

"Cops & Doughnuts," he said, forcing a cheerful tone he didn't feel.

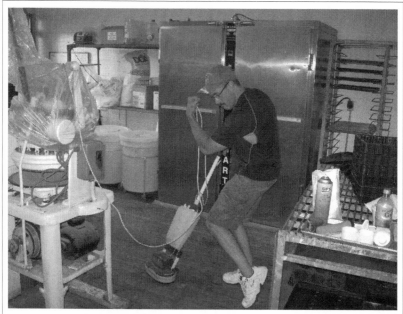

Dogman mopping up at closing time—with flair!

"Hello, this is Fox News and we'd like to do a story about your bakery."

Bubba thought it was the local Fox affiliate. But then the reporter offered to send a limousine to take the nine cops to the TV station in Flint, Michigan.

Bubba was just now sensing it wasn't the Fox local affiliate. Could it be . . . *Fox and Friends*, the national show? Yes indeed! But the starstruck Bubba explained the situation.

"If you're sending a limousine to take us down there, you can't get all nine of us. Someone's gotta stay in town. You want all nine, you come here."

The producer promised to see what he could do and called back a few minutes later.

"I'm canceling the limousine . . ." he said.

"Oh, shoot," Bubba thought. "I messed up."

"I got a satellite truck. We'll be there tomorrow morning at 5:30, and it would be great if you could get a crowd of people together."

Bubba relievedly agreed, hung up, and told Beaver and Ryno the good news. The three cops drove directly from the bakery to the city commission meeting, where they announced the news.

"Fox News is coming and we gotta make sure the bakery's full tomorrow morning because we're going to be on *Fox and Friends*. We need everybody to show up first thing," Ryno told the crowd.

Meantime, the cop owners got on the phone and called every person they knew.

The next morning, scores of people had lined up at the door at 5:30 a.m. to greet the Fox News satellite truck. A

COPS & DOUGHNUTS

Top: The Fox News satellite truck beams news of Clare and its new bakery. Bottom: Hurry up and wait. Dogman and his fellow cop owners wait hours for the *Fox and Friends* interview.

producer, a soundman, and a cameraman clambered out of their car, impressed by the strong turnout. They quickly got to work, hauling in lights to brighten the bakery. They gathered the cops and posed them carefully around the glass cases of doughnuts.

Dogman was first in line and outfitted with an earpiece that connected to the *Fox & Friends* news set in New York (none of the other cops could hear the interview). The cops had decided earlier that he would be the face of Cops & Doughnuts for the interview since he was a perfect cop specimen—good-looking guy, fit, and just the right age.

All was set to go, but the producer announced to the crowd and cops that a breaking news story was pushing back the segment. The same thing happened every fifteen minutes. Every time it looked like they'd get the go-ahead, another news story popped. As the hours went by, the temperature soared, and the cops felt a little fried.

"They had it so hot in there, we were sweating like pigs. No pun intended," Ryno said.

Now as the clock ticked toward 9:00 a.m., the ending time for the three-hour show, the cops grew anxious.

"We're not going to get on, are we?" Ryno asked the producer.

"You'll get on; they spent a lot of money to get us here," he said.

"How much time are we going to get?"

"Probably ninety seconds is about it, *if* things work out," the producer said. "You'll get at least one commercial lead-in and maybe two."

Finally, at 8:45 a.m., they were on!

COPS & DOUGHNUTS

"I had no clue at that time, just what this meant. I never had any issues talking in front of large groups," Dogman said. "But it was funny, just before we go on, they said, 'Are you ready for this?' I said, 'Sure, it's a piece of cake.' 'Okay, you're going to be in front of twenty million people; I just want you to know.' That kind of hit home. I thought, it seemed impossible that our bakery was going to be thrust into the national limelight that quickly."

Fox News hosts Eric Bolling and Brian Kilmeade conducted the interview, asking Dogman if the cops were getting doughnuts for free. "Actually," he explained, "we don't get free doughnuts. We put our money in the till just like everybody else, so we're not eating up our profits." And then poking fun at the stereotype, Kilmeade asked if the cops had "gotten fatter" since they opened. Dogman laughed. "You know what? We've been so busy we've had some guys lose some weight."

As it turns out, the clip lasted three minutes and fifteen seconds.

Sadly, the crowd—for all of the time they patiently waited on the sidewalk—wasn't included in the segment, but the station provided the raw news footage to every Fox affiliate in the country.

The excitement over, the producer motioned Ryno over to the satellite truck. He pointed to the multiple TV screens, specifically, the CNN station that was now teasing upcoming news: "Later this morning, the story of how cops save a bakery in a small Michigan town."

CNN had decided it was a story after all.

Chapter 2

THE HIDDEN
BROTHERHOOD OF COPS

With such a spectacular kickoff, the bakery was turning a solid profit over the next several years, and Bubba and Ryno decided to retire early in 2013 to run the bakery full-time. They walked away from the stress of police work but not from their nearly sixty combined years of memories—cabin burglaries, meth labs exploding in the middle of nowhere, pulling over argumentative drivers, breaking up domestic disputes, and (for Bubba) serving as a school liaison.

Now their attention was turned to spreadsheets, brainstorming marketing and merchandising ideas, and their most challenging task—finding good help in a tightening job market.

But for Bubba, the memories of criminal investigations still stuck with him, especially sexual assaults against youth. For eighteen years, he had handled every criminal sexual allegation that came into the Clare Police Department. He also traversed the state as a consultant, training other officers how to investigate sexual assaults of children.

"When I see a fifty-five-year-old man walking down the street with an eight-year-old, I don't think, 'Isn't that nice, Grandpa is taking his little granddaughter out for an ice cream.' That is not my first thought."

COPS & DOUGHNUTS

Bubba said police work leaves a person with a distorted perception of the world. Criminals comprise only a small percentage of the population, but a cop spends nearly his or her entire day dealing with lawbreakers.

That kind of intense stress for decades can take its toll on an officer's psyche and his or her outlook on the world, Dogman said.

"We regularly see the worst of the worst, but the reality is they are only a small percentage. From the trailer park to the half-a-million-dollar home, we see people at their worst, and they all want us to solve their problems," Dogman said.

Michigan State Police troopers Mike White and Tim Cruttenden from the Mt. Pleasant post pose for a photo before going inside for a doughnut and coffee. Trooper White has since passed away.

Since the bakery first opened in 2009, police officers have gravitated to the bakery, some out of curiosity, others to share their work stories over a cup of coffee.

"We understand each other," Dogman said. "When you tell something to a friend who is not in the business, they don't quite get it. When you talk to guys who jumped in the same fire, they get it."

When off-duty cops walk through the door, Bubba said he can spot them instantly.

"I'll walk up to them. 'Pardon me, what department are you with?' And nine out of ten times, I'm right. They're an off-duty cop. It's just the way they act, the way they look. No cop shaves on his day off. If you gotta guy walking in here with a relatively

Retired cops chat at the roundtable with family and friends.

short haircut, unshaven, he's wearing loose-fitting pants, and his shirt isn't tucked in, you know he's a cop."

A female off-duty cop will wear her hair down—on duty, it must be tightly tied up. She won't carry a gun inside her waistband, but in her purse or a leather pouch on her side. She'll wear loose clothing—it helps if she finds herself in a fight. She'll also be assertive.

"It's a cop thing," Bubba said.

To the casual onlooker, cops might look relaxed, but they sit with their back to the wall, scanning the room and sizing up who's walking through the door. Most carry a concealed weapon, Bubba said, including himself.

Visiting officers often gather at a weathered roundtable that looks out onto the main street of Clare. Above the table is a large, horizontal sign: "OLD COOTS GIVING ADVICE: It's probably bad advice, but it's free." They keep the conversation light, preferring to keep the disturbing stories of work to themselves, Ryno said.

"We like to forget and move on. We might talk about a funny story, but nothing that affected us traumatically. We're not good about talking about those things," he said.

Yet the roundtable is where off-duty cops can go to guard against the cynicism that comes with the job, said Josh Lator, who goes way back with Ryno and Bubba. He worked with them for years when he was a Michigan State Police trooper with the Mount Pleasant post. He backed them up on calls and they did the same. Over time, he became a close friend with Bubba and his family.

At six-foot-four and a lean 285 pounds, he cuts a commanding force and the Clare cops would often call him to break down a door (legally), when necessary—Josh's nickname was "Key to the City." But he's also well-read, consuming several psychology and leadership books a month. Now the commander of Mount Pleasant Post #63, he knows that psychological injuries from the job must be treated with as much respect as physical wounds.

Josh explained that in the olden days, a trooper who experienced a "bad day" was encouraged to go home and have a drink. Maybe two. Now they're offered therapeutic counsel and a couple of days off to regroup.

"With a traumatic event, you get all these higher levels of chemicals dumped into your brain. By the time you get to the end of your shift, you are just coming down so you don't have mental stability. Then you go home, whether you have a wife and family, you're drinking alcohol, which dulls it for a time, but actually makes it worse in the morning because your chemical balance is even more off. With the chemicals in your head, you have to hit REM sleep one full sleep cycle, at least, for your brain to reset. Unless you do that, now you're not reset and you're emotional.

"So, the next day, you still feel like crap. 'I'm not me. I guess I'll have another beer.' And you're just constantly trying to regulate what's up here with what's out there. It doesn't work.

"No one back in the day was saying, 'Let's take three days off. Go home, take your wife out to dinner, sleep, go talk to the dog, talk to a chaplain, and I'll come over off duty, and we'll sit on your back porch and you just tell me whatever you need.' That didn't happen. And so, these officers had no support network and they were never taught how to, in a healthy way, work through the psychological aspect. And families didn't get an explanation either about what was going on with their loved one."

Bubba said that Josh was there for him, when he got a call on a child who passed away during the night.

"When I arrived, the child was already in rigor mortis, and the family freaked out. I did CPR on a child long dead—you can't not just do something, even when there's no hope. I could still remember the smell of her days later. I remember reaching out to Josh, and we had a counseling session. It helped me . . . a lot. We are really, really close friends."

So, what does this have to do with the Cops & Doughnuts' roundtable? Josh explained that gathering at the bakery reflects an evolving openness toward sharing feelings and camaraderie.

Cops & Doughnuts welcomes cops from all corners.

"One of the things that happens when you get retirees, on-duty police officers, and new police officers all together at the roundtable, is they develop a common trust with each other," Josh said. "And when you have trust, you can be honest about what you're struggling with. At that roundtable, someone may not talk about the fact that they're having a really tough time, but they might have a relaxed conversation that leads to a conversation at a later time in private," he said. "If you weren't sitting at that table having a cup of coffee, that conversation may have never come up.

"That roundtable is kind of unintentionally symbolic of that brotherhood of law enforcement. If I go in there and I sit down, there may be a retired chief and his wife. There may be Bubba and Ryno sitting there. There may be a retired DNR officer. There may be a couple of on-duty guys there. For a young police officer, they realize 'I get to sit in the presence of these senior guys and learn from them and hear their stories, and feel that I'm being included as that new guy, and these older guys are setting the standard for what's expected of me.'

"If you're the on-duty guy that's been there awhile, you can be kind of relaxed. You can be around some brothers if you've had a good day or a bad day. It's just a hot cup of coffee and a good conversation. When a retiree comes and sits down at that table, they know they're respected for who they are. They're respected for what they've done. And it's a way they can still stay connected to that team environment and brotherhood. There's guys there that have been retired twenty years and they get the same reception as the guy that's been on duty for ten years."

Cops riding on the East Lansing Motor Training Ride make a doughnut stop in Clare.

COPS & DOUGHNUTS

The roundtable isn't reserved for just officers. Anyone can pull up a chair and they often do.

"People [who live in Clare] know that when they walk into the bakery, there's going to be this open communication and everybody's welcome," Josh said. "There are people that come up to the table and say, 'Sorry to bother you guys, but I have a police question and you've kind of got what we call the "brain trust" sitting there.' No one ever tells them, 'Don't interrupt us. We're talking.' It's, 'Hey, how are you? How are you doing? Where are you from?' And nothing is off limits. 'Just ask a question, I'll give you an honest answer.' So that's the cool thing about that table."

Josh said that his son, who grew up hunting and fishing with Bubba, is now a conservation officer and a brother in blue.

"It's interesting. They treated him very well when he was just a young man in the community, and now they have taken him in as a brother-in-arms. It's neat to see that come full circle."

One of the farthest-flung visitors was David Kniesz, who worked as a tourist police officer in Thailand. He visited the bakery in 2011.

"He was being paid by church missionaries who put guys like him to work as reserve police officers to take photographic evidence of U.S. people buying girls and boys for the sex trade. He would share the photos with the feds, and under U.S. law, they could make arrests.

"We have pictures of David and the other guys with their T-shirts and guerrilla camouflage and rifles—they were going on a search to find victims. They'd find and rescue whole families where they would hide them in sewers. The missionary bought a multistory building, so the women could live and work there.

They thought they could bring in a Cops & Doughnuts operation where they could learn the skills to make product and raise money for the shelter, but we couldn't make it work with all the international rules."

POLICING THE MEMORABILIA

Walk into the bakery and you might feel overwhelmed with the sheer amount of memorabilia. It's on every single wall and every nook and cranny. It's a rare day when a visiting cop hasn't stopped by to share a story or present a gift of appreciation.

"People just started showing up, saying 'I appreciate what you do' and giving us a shoulder patch. We never asked for it. They just showed up. We have a whole bunch of those now. It's a police thing," Bubba said.

In fact, the bakery has more than 3,000 shoulder patches from different agencies, said Ryno.

"In the beginning we kept an alphabetical book. For every patch given to us, we gave them one of our Cops & Doughnuts shoulder patches. It's slowed down enough, but we'll still take one, especially if they've traveled far enough and we don't already have one," Bubba said.

"Some of this stuff is technically stolen property, although it's not worth anything," Bubba added. "We've got two doors off sheriff's department vehicles that were in a wreck. Some guy salvaged one of them and brought it in, saying, 'Here's a piece of a wrecked door.' Another door was left in the alley behind the bakery, and we picked it up and brought it in."

Once cops see what the bakery is all about, they'll return with something that's been in their man cave for years, Bubba said.

"They think, 'Nobody's seeing this but me, so I will donate

27

it.' We've got an old Breathalyzer that a cop was given for a retirement gift. We get a lot of challenge coins. It's a military thing, and the police are a paramilitary organization. In the military, if you do something really good, above and beyond, a commanding officer may reward you with a coin with their unit's name on it."

People have brought in cop figurines and cookie jars. In 2014, a young soldier brought in a folded U.S. flag that once flew over a military base in Afghanistan. One day, Ryno opened the mail and found a Metropolitan Police helmet shipped by a former police officer living in the Shetland Islands. He had started a friendship over shortwave radio with a Michigan man, and they had both visited the Clare Headquarters.

A retired Detroit police officer brought in a call box that officers would use to reach another officer for backup. When the department switched to portable radios in the 1960s, the Detroit officers were encouraged to pick up the boxes and take them home.

"A retired officer did that, and he gave it to us. He had it in his home for many, many years," Ryno said.

A family of a Detroit cop in 2011 brought in a huge photo of Officer Daniel Lindsley seated on a Detroit Police Department motorcycle. A few months later, a couple of family members returned, anxious to see the photo hanging on the wall. Unfortunately, it had been taken down a few weeks before and rotated down to the basement to make room for another picture.

"They told us, 'Hey, we gave you that picture to be on display. If you're not going to put it up, we'll take it home,'" Ryno said, adding that the problem was immediately rectified. "How you handle all of this can get sensitive."

Ryno wants the bakery to be an upbeat place, so memorials and tributes to fallen officers aren't a focus. But there are exceptions. A family came into the bakery in 2011 to talk about the life of their son, Bryan Gross.

"He was a young police officer from the Midland area, and he really wanted to move out west to Converse, Colorado," Ryno said. "He met a girl out there and fell in love with her. Mom and Grandma moved out to be near him, and in this picture here, he's standing in front of his patrol truck. There's a little log cabin church behind him. They had just had a wedding in that mountain church."

In July 2011, the officer and others in his unit had been called out to rescue a woman, who had thrown herself into the river, trying to commit suicide.

"They saved the girl, but when everyone was back on shore, he wasn't with them. This young deputy had drowned in the North Platte River, trying to rescue her. The officer's family was from the Gladwin area, and they brought that story along with his photo and obituary eight years ago. Since then, the sheriff from Converse County took a vacation and came here to see where the photo is displayed."

THE BACKSTORY OF DOUGHNUTS & COPS

Although many cops are drawn to the bakery, not all cops buy into the stereotype of cops and doughnuts and weren't thrilled with the Clare cops poking fun at themselves.

The stereotype of cops hanging out at doughnut shops has a historical basis. Cops first became bakery regulars beginning in the 1950s—and for good reason—they were one of the few places in sync with the cops' schedules—open late at night and early in the morning. Buying a doughnut and coffee didn't cost much, still doesn't, and it was a quick way to get an energy jolt during a long night in the cruiser. And what better comfort food after a night of boredom or a tough encounter?

But a lot of cops find the stereotype insulting.

"You know, I've never eaten a doughnut in uniform because I made a promise in the police academy because of the stereotype that it held, of course. I made that promise, not knowing that I would eventually be a part owner of a bakery," said Rich "Junior" Ward. "So, in any of our photo ops, I hold a cookie instead.

"Most of the younger generation of cops took it for what it was, which was just, if anybody is going to make fun of us, we can because we are police officers. You know, if you had a group of defense attorneys that bought the bakery and called it cops and doughnuts, there'd be more offense taken."

Rich remembers he was sitting in his car running stationary radar when a man walked up holding a box of doughnuts from the bakery.

"I don't want to stereotype, but I just got these and they're super good. Do you want one? They're from Cops & Doughnuts," he said.

"I appreciate it," Ward said. "I really do. But I'm also an owner, so I've eaten many of those. I'd rather you enjoy them than me."

Some cops took offense to the logo—a white-frosted doughnut wrapped around a police badge, Ryno said.

"They thought it was a disgrace to the badge. Some of the younger guys, guys in good shape, said, 'You'll never catch me with a doughnut in my hand.' But once we explained it, they accepted it. They got older and wiser and saw how we've given back to the community."

Retired Michigan State trooper Tim Cruttenden, who worked with the Clare cops over the years, caught heat from his Mount Pleasant colleagues for enjoying a doughnut at the bakery on opening day. He drove over to Clare while off duty and left with a box of doughnuts for his fellow troopers. He told the *Morning Sun* reporter, "They're yummy," a comment for which he was nicknamed "Trooper Yummy."

"Some cops are sensitive about the stereotype. But I still think it was a great idea when you see all the good they've done," Tim said.

Tim doesn't get to the bakery very often; he now lives and works processing case evidence at a police department forty miles away. But he remembers a time back in 2009, when he and Clare Police Officer Brian Gregory, the Clare canine officer at the time, were trying to track down a runaway suspect in nearby Farwell.

Michigan State Police trooper Tim Cruttenden.

"I made a friendly wager, betting an apple fritter, that we don't find him," he said. Tim won. "That night, the guy got away."

DRAWING COPS TOGETHER

In 2015 or so, troopers from both sides of the Mackinac Bridge decided to meet up at the bakery to celebrate their 50th birthdays with friends and family.

COPS & DOUGHNUTS

"They didn't even check with us, but they know how open we are with cops. They just showed up with balloons and gifts," Ryno said.

Cops also fraternize on the Cops & Doughnuts Facebook pages—there have been literally tens of thousands of posts over the years, said Ryno.

"You could spend a year reading through it," said Ryno, who, in fact, does spend four hours a day, seven days a week, responding to messages.

The Cops & Doughnuts police owners have traveled to Washington, D.C. for National Police Week, where they've taken bags of Cops & Doughnuts shoulder patches to trade. Cops don't make it a practice to celebrate themselves, so it's a rare opportunity to enjoy the camaraderie, Beaver said.

"It's a hidden brotherhood. It's not like firefighters. Firefighters are very open about who they are—they wear T-shirts, they

Facebook photos of the Cops & Doughnuts van in Washington, D.C.

put bumper stickers on their cars—because they're all considered heroes. It's not the same for cops, although that's started to change in the last ten years," Beaver said.

From early on, Ryno and Bubba figured out that doughnuts and the Second Amendment worked pretty well together. They had made the decision to open a substation inside of Ace Hardware and Sports in Midland where customers will find a gleaming glass case filled with shelves of doughnuts, delivered fresh each day. On one occasion, a customer took a picture of the doughnuts with the gun section of the store in the background. He wrote: "My politics are whatever this is."

"His post just went viral," Ryno said. "Without exaggeration, millions of people have seen it. It got so many shares, it was goofy."

Gun afficionados are also part of the brotherhood. Bob Snapp, for example, was a regular at the roundtable of Cops & Doughnuts. He had gained a national reputation for his

The late Bob Snapp, a bakery regular, is honored by a mounted caribou he shot in Canada with his custom rifle.

custom-made rifles and handguns, but retirement left a work-shaped hole in his life and he needed a place to go. Cops & Doughnuts became his refuge. Every day, for hours a day, you'd find him at the roundtable, basking in the company of the bakery regulars and the staff, who always made a fuss over him. As he got older and his health weakened, Bubba and Ryno kept a close eye on him.

"We had a rule that if he wasn't going to come in, he had to call us," Bubba said. "We told him, 'If you're not here by 11 o'clock and we don't hear your call for a while, we'll call you. And if you don't answer, we're going to check you out.' We knew where he lived and how to get in the house, and we did go in many, many times."

When Bob ultimately became housebound, Ryno and Bubba helped his family find an assisted living facility. He later passed away in January of 2019, said Ann Rodgers, his daughter.

In honor of Bob, the bakery displays a mounted head of a caribou that Bob had killed in Canada's Northwest Territories with his custom rifle.

"The head had hung in his dining room. For years. It's huge. The living room had just a regular ceiling height and the thing practically reached the ground," Rodgers said.

The family wanted the bakery to have the head as a permanent reminder of Bob. But he needed a name, Bubba said.

"So, Bob's legal name was Robert Joseph, and he had a nickname of Bobby Joe, but he hated being called that. Only his wife was allowed to call him that. So, of course, we named the caribou head Bobby Joe," Bubba said.

Ryno and Bubba and Beaver miss their old friend Bob Snapp, but there's still Bobby Joe, his glass eyes gazing at the roundtable where Bob once chatted and laughed with friends.

Chapter 3

COPS AND KINDNESS

On a hot summer day, a Clare cop was on patrol and noticed a run-down car slowly driving through town. The tires were bald, the exhaust hissing, the entire car pockmarked with rust.

The cop switched on his siren to a two-tone yelp and pulled the car over. The officer walked up to the driver's window and introduced himself to a young mom and said hello to the two little kids in tow.

He explained that she was operating an unsafe vehicle. He gave her a warning instead of a ticket, which would have meant she'd have two weeks to get the car repaired or face a big "or else"—a fine and a suspended driver's license. The latter usually creates even more problems, as in no way to get to work, and it was obvious this particular woman didn't have a dollar in her wallet. So, the cop—a bakery owner—called Ryno and Bubba to see if Cops & Doughnuts could help out.

"He was worried that she'd get in an accident—the tires were extremely dangerous. There was also the chance of carbon monoxide leaking into the car and poisoning anyone inside. So, I said, 'Yes, tell her to take the car to a repair shop in Clare. I'll call them and ask 'em to put on a decent set of tires and get the car roadworthy and to send us the invoice,'" Bubba said.

COPS & DOUGHNUTS

The years of robust profits from Cops & Doughnuts have provided the bakery with a small fund to help people like that single mom. And the relationship between the bakery and the cop owners on the road has created a perfect synergy: the cop-owned bakery is only a phone call away from the cops on patrol.

But Bubba said that long before Cops & Doughnuts existed, he and the Clare cops helped people, on duty and off.

One afternoon, for example, the Clare Police Department got a call from a guy who had hit a deer with his car and wanted to take it home. The young man had a hunting permit in his possession but no idea of how to field dress the deer—to remove its intestines, which needs to be done immediately.

"I drove over to help him out, but I myself didn't gut it—I had my uniform on. But I stood there and told him step-by-step how to do it," Bubba said.

In another case, an older woman called the Clare cops almost weekly to report suspicious noises outside her home.

"We'd get over there and look around and knock on the door and tell her we didn't see anything. So, then she'd invite us in for milk and cookies. We'd sit for fifteen, twenty minutes talking with her. She was lonely, and that's all she really wanted."

One night, Bubba and his partner were out patrolling, when a call came in at ten from grandkids, saying their grandparents weren't answering their phone.

"They're calling and calling and calling and want us to see if they're all right," Bubba said. "We call that a welfare check. We knock and the couple comes to the door. They're both eighty-five. When they saw us, they light up like a Christmas tree. The next thing you know, they're saying, 'Come in officers,' and make us coffee and set out plates of apple pie. They were so happy to have visitors at ten at night. We tried to leave, but we were there for forty-five minutes."

Helping with emergency car problems has always been a big one—from getting under the hood to fix a fuse to helping a driver who's run out of gas. Sometimes a cop will even pitch in twenty dollars from their own pocket for gas.

Yet during these undeniably fraught times in our country, one hears little about the kindness of cops. The nation's attention instead has focused largely on cover-ups of bad actors, racism, and jury trials of officers who have killed someone in the line of duty.

Police officers rarely get the attention for their acts of kindness because the public isn't aware of them—and that's because officers generally don't talk about their good deeds, said Joshua Lator, commander of the Michigan State Police Mount Pleasant post.

> "We're small-town cops. We live in the community. We have a vested interest in treating people with respect and fairness."
> —Bubba

"Anti-police sentiment gets clicks on social media, but you usually don't hear about police officers who are very, very quick to help, even outside of law enforcement. If they see a need, they will find a way to get help, even if it's not a physical need they can meet right away," Josh said.

He cited an example of a cop who knew a parent whose child was having a mental crisis and couldn't get help.

"A call went out to the prosecuting attorney, to other police officers, to behavioral scientists with my department and within a matter of a couple of hours, we had someone that said, 'You have him call me and I'll get him connected with the right people.' Even that's meeting a need in your community. But he wasn't on duty. No one was getting paid for it.

Police officers, along with teachers, are the ones left to deal with society's shortcomings. The needs are great and the funds are short to help those who are homeless, suicidal, or barely getting by. With the closure of Michigan's mental health institutions and methamphetamine labs dotting the rural countryside, cops must cope with the fallout of addiction and untreated mental illness. Many of their calls are related to folks who can barely get by.

Ryno remembers an incident of a woman leaving her home to spend time with some friends. When she returned home several hours later, she found her husband dead in their queen-size bed, the mattress soaked with urine and feces—a natural occurrence of death.

When Brian "Dogman" Gregory responded to her 9-1-1 call, the woman asked him if he could help flip over the mattress. She told him she couldn't afford to buy a new one, prompting Gregory to call to Cops & Doughnuts.

"Hey, guys, can we help this elderly lady here?" he asked. "Her husband passed away late in bed one night. There's fluids all over the mattress and she can't afford to buy another one. She said she's planning on wrapping it with plastic, putting her sheets back on, and sleeping on it tonight."

Bubba and Ryno talked it over and decided the bakery had to help. Bubba called the furniture store.

"'Hey, somebody has passed away, and we need you to take over a brand-new mattress and pick up the old one. Send us the bill.' We've done this a couple of times."

Bubba remembers a call that came in around midnight. He

was on duty and the station got a call from a single mom whose son was eight years old. He woke up from a terrifying nightmare, and she couldn't console him. She thought an officer could help. Bubba remembers arriving at a rundown two-bedroom house that smelled of cigarette smoke—just the mom and boy lived there. She showed him to the bedroom of the boy, the wallpaper covered in astronauts. He was still crying.

"I came over and sat on his bed and talked to him and talked to him about things that are real and not real. I comforted him until he was calmed down enough to go back to sleep," said Bubba.

"Police work is as much social work as anything else, and we're the ones out on the line every day, twenty-four seven. We're small-town cops. We live in the community. We have a vested interest in treating people with respect and fairness."

Bubba said that the cops just seem to folks more approachable when they're working inside a bakery.

Bubba said having worked thirty years as a cop, he's fully aware of the hardship of financial duress, and the last thing he wants to do is write a ticket.

"I always call a traffic stop an adult time-out. 'You were doing something bad, and now you're going to have a time-out.' But in a small town, we live here, too. I used to tell the young officers, you might be stopping a kid's teacher, the guy who rings up your gas or fixes your car—we all have to get along. I'm not out there to punish somebody for being poor. The poor are the most exploited people in the world."

In one instance of kicking people when they're already down, the local newspaper reported that someone stole a portable aluminum ramp from a house outside of Clare in the middle of the night. Presumably they wanted it for the value of aluminum, but it left the elderly couple in wheelchairs without a way to get in and out of the house. Bubba called the editor and asked for the couple's address.

"Why do you want to know?" the editor asked.

"Well, Cops & Doughnuts is going to install a new ramp for them, and I have to know if they're going to be there."

Bubba recalls another time when a young mom brought her clearly shaken little boy to the Cops & Doughnuts bakery. He took the boy to the doughnut case and said he could pick out his favorite one. Then he took the mom to a quiet table, where she told him that her boyfriend had sexually assaulted her son in her Isabella County home, some fifteen miles away. Her son was too scared to meet with an officer, but said he'd talk to the guys at Cops & Doughnuts because they were nice.

Bubba sat down with the boy and talked with him for a while, calming him down.

"I told him I had a friend I'd like him to meet. 'He's a police officer, he can help you, and I know you can trust him.'"

When the boy agreed, Bubba called for a detective from the Michigan State Police post to meet the boy at the bakery and take him to the police station, where he could be interviewed and recorded.

Little kids are not the only ones who feel like cops are more approachable when they're working inside a bakery.

"I've had people I've arrested come and have a doughnut with me. When you arrest people in a small town, you know them and treat them with dignity and respect."

In another police-related matter, a man—a father in the community—had failed to take care of a traffic ticket and he received a letter reading that a warrant had been issued for his arrest. Now he feared he would be pulled over with both his children in the car. Wanting to save himself and his kids the embarrassment, he walked into the bakery shortly after 4 p.m. and turned himself in.

Bubba remembers helping out a young couple who lost their two-year-old son. Bubba called the funeral home as soon as he heard the tragic news.

"I told them, 'I want you to give this family a nice funeral and just send me the bill for it,'" he said. "The father had run over his two-year-old. He was, as you can imagine, inconsolable."

"Everything good in the community that occurs, the cops are [in] some way involved."
—Former City Manager Ken Hibl

The cops are not only known for small deeds, but for some very big ones, too. They have helped transform Clare into a bustling downtown by supporting area businesses, youth groups, and nonprofits. Ryno serves on the Downtown Development Authority, is a longtime member of the Rotary Club, and executive board member of Middle Michigan Development Corporation.

"Everything good in the community that occurs, the cops are [in] some way involved," said former City Manager Ken Hibl. "They were instrumental in creating Art Alley. They helped support the railroad depot project—the roof of the old depot was falling in and the town was able to save it. . . .

COPS & DOUGHNUTS

They helped us fundraise close to a million dollars to renovate it, including the sweat equity."

Cops & Doughnuts has committed all kinds of generous acts since opening their doors in 2009. Here are a few of them:

- The cop owners decided to throw a lot of support to the jazz band, realizing the musicians don't get as much attention or funding as the sports programs. For a few years, the cops donated catered food and a nice venue for the band's annual fundraiser. In truth, it was a selfish move—they had suffered through years of cheap meals in the school cafeteria and wanted something delicious in a comfortable place for a change.
- The cops buy a hog each year from a 4-H member and promptly return it to him or her to keep as a pet. Except that one summer when a little boy's parent said no to a pet goat. The bakery nearly gained an unwanted mascot, but someone at the fair stepped forward and volunteered to take it home.
- Each year, the cop owners supply doughnut holes for the high school's homecoming bonfire. They promote blood drives at the Red Cross and provide doughnuts for donors. They paid for the city's larger, prettier street signs. And the bakery annually sponsors a T-ball team because everybody is happy in T-ball. The coaches don't keep score and nobody yells at the coaches, kids or each other.
- One year, Cops & Doughnuts sponsored all 30 youth soccer teams, buying shirts for all of them when the league was having trouble finding a sponsor. Cops & Doughnuts played Cops & Doughnuts for the entire season.

- Cops & Doughnuts keeps cables and tools on hand to help anyone stranded in front with a dead battery or locked car.
- Bubba hosts tours of the bakery for homeschoolers.
- Cops & Doughnuts supports a summer reading program, giving kids one doughnut for every book they read.
- The bakery donates plants and flowers for city landscaping and hires bands to perform in the downtown area.
- When the power goes out, the cops can rely on a monster generator to keep the bakery in operation. Nearby businesses are invited to plug in an extension cord to keep their own businesses going.
- Cops & Doughnuts bakers need to fry up enough doughnuts for the three other precincts and nine substations. Because the bakers are cooking 24/7, the cops have an open-door policy for all the snowplow drivers needing a place to warm up, a steaming cup of coffee, and a bathroom break.
- Cops came to the rescue of JT Bakers, a family-owned bakery that planned to move from Alma into Clare around the corner from Cops & Doughnuts in 2010, a year after the nine cop owners had set up shop. The cop owners were initially alarmed, but then learned JT Bakers was a wholesaler that sold bread, wedding cakes, and other bakery goods to grocery stores and restaurants. As it turns out, JT Bakers discovered there was a two-month delay on its new location, so the cop owners invited them to use the back of their bakery during off-hours.

COPS & DOUGHNUTS

In 2013, JT Bakers needed help again. It lost power just an hour before hundreds of loaves were ready to go in the oven. Cops & Doughnuts came to the rescue, loaning its ovens just in the nick of time.

- Cops & Doughnuts always makes a good story and is frequently called by TV 9&10 News. Bubba and Ryno often share the spotlight and call other business owners to join the media spotlight.

There are other small things that don't cost money. For one, the bakery is a popular meeting place for Bible study groups, creative types, old high school chums, and people meeting a person they met online for the first time.

"A woman wants a safe place and what could be safer than a bakery owned by nine cops where there are always cops around?" Bubba said.

"One evening, I had this woman come in, she was seventy-five, all dolled up, hair all done up. She got a coffee and sat down at this table. Working as a cop for thirty years, I could tell she was upset about something. I asked her, 'Is everything okay?' She said, 'I met a gentleman online and I've never done anything like this before, but I wanted to meet him and I'm really nervous. You know, you never know if they are who say they are.'"

So, Bubba sat down with her to help her wait for her date. Soon, an eighty-year-old with an oxygen mask hobbled over and sat down.

"He didn't look like much of a threat. They spent an hour talking and giggling like school kids."

Ryno and Bubba freely admit they're complete hams and will do goofy stuff no one else would dare—and then make a video post to Facebook and Instagram. Case in point—they

Alumni from the class of 1967 meet up in the bakery about once a month.

wanted to promote two good causes: a furniture store sales event and March is Reading Month for kids. They came up with what was admittedly their most outrageous stunt yet.

COPS & DOUGHNUTS

"We walked down to the Woods Household furniture store, and I sat down in a big recliner and Ryno sits in my lap. And on video, I read *Green Eggs and Ham*. We have no shame."

The video went on Facebook and Instagram, drawing thousands of hits. And the furniture store now had video proof that their La-Z-Boy recliners could support serious poundage.

Bubba remembers when the new owner of the Timeout Tavern across the street completely remodeled the restaurant. Bubba and Ryno walked over to visit and take a look around.

"They were just ready to have a soft opening, and we went over and were looking around."

"I think we'll be ready tomorrow night to open," said owner Dave Maxwell. "Could you guys do a video and put it on Facebook and help us get people in?"

"Are you sure," said Ryno, "because if we do, we'll flood this place. Are you *really* ready because we've got 66,000 followers—a lot of people will see it."

"We're ready," the owner insisted.

So, the post went up and the restaurant was beyond swamped.

"It blew them away. They had people lined up outside. They said, 'Man, you guys weren't kidding.'"

"We told ya!"

Tour buses line McEwan Street in the summer months.

If you're a Clare business and need help with publicity, Bubba said, "all you have to do is ask and we'll come do a video."

In 2018 he posted on social media that $8,000 more was needed to finish the depot and advertised a red-hot special on "depot cookies," priced from $2 to $1,000 apiece. They sold several for $1,000, including two to the same guy, and raised $7,469 in eight hours.

The restored railroad depot is now home to Clare's chamber of commerce and arts council.

More than anything, the bakery has brought cars and customers to Clare.

"Tour buses have Cops & Doughnuts on their agendas to come visit. Pre-pandemic, it was about 100 tour buses a year. They park on the street and the tourists get off. In the

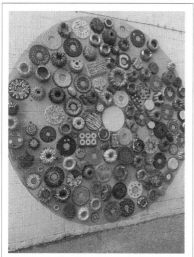

One of many colorful murals in Art Alley, which you'll find right behind the bakery.

What's an Art Alley without a little cop humor?

summertime, it's not uncommon to see the line going into the bakery all the way down the street," said former City Manager Ken Hibl.

The cop owners may look like tough guys, but they are one of the biggest supporters of arts and culture. For one, the Arts Council. The bakery was approached by artists who wanted to transform the alley, most of it behind their three buildings. The plan was to call it Art Alley. The cop owners immediately agreed, and the artists painted brilliantly colored, whimsical murals. Their dream came true, and now it's a hot spot for tourist photo-taking.

"Last year, they hosted a country music party in the alley. They were a big part of that. The stage was in the alley right behind the bakery and blocked off. Bubba and Ryno took the stage in back of their building," said Jeremy Howard, Clare city manager.

Ken added that "Cops & Doughnuts is helping in doing an art walk in Clare, so again it all fits together."

Clare has one of the best football complexes in the state with artificial turf—it's a popular choice in the state for football and soccer teams that need a neutral place to compete. Whenever teams are scheduled to play a big game, Ryno puts ads on Facebook that reach anyone living within twenty miles of the two competing cities—"Hey, if you're coming to Clare for the football game, check out our great restaurants and things to do!" In addition, any visitor to any sporting event that asks for a coffee or hot chocolate receives it in a Cops & Doughnut cup.

The customers can also be kind. Once, when Ryno was working the counter, Bernie Davison, a regular customer and veteran, arrived at the counter at the same time as three local teen boys. One of the younger boys paid for Bernie's doughnut and his buddies' doughnuts to boot. Bernie was honored, and the story landed on a Facebook post on the AskMidland page.

"Someone raised that boy right," she wrote.

In 2022, Bubba and Ryno took their goodwill on the road and set up a roving "roundtable" in partnership with 9&10 News in Cadillac. Their prime destination: the place in town where old curmudgeons meet and gossip.

"The bakery's roundtable comes from the [now closed] Lone Pine Restaurant, and it has been a gathering place at Cops & Doughnuts for a lot of years. We wanted to celebrate that, so what we do is ask people to nominate their favorite community table.

"The first month we had 170 nominations. This month, we had 300 and some."

Once the winner is picked, the cops make a visit with a miniature version of the banner that hangs in the bakery: "OLD COOTS GIVE ADVICE: It's probably bad advice, but it's free."

On each visit, the bakery also identifies a project in need.

"Our first check was to a roller-skating rink that had been in Cadillac since Hector was a pup. It burned down and people are trying to get it back for the kids," Bubba said.

The cops donate one hundred dollars on each visit—admittedly, not that much money—but the feelings they leave behind are worth pure gold.

Not all good deeds change lives, but some do—even small deeds like shipping out doughnuts to a man who is desperately fighting for his life.

Bubba and Ryno recounted the story of Major Jon Turnbull,

COPS & DOUGHNUTS

Bernie Davison, a bakery regular
and veteran, gained a bit of
notoriety on Facebook.

who was critically wounded in
Manbij, Syria, after an ISIS suicide bomber blew himself up in
front of a restaurant and next to
a school where Jon and his patrol
had just delivered aid, he wrote in
his memoir, *Zero Percent Chance*.

The bomb killed three Americans, dozens of Syrian civilians,
a linguist, and five others who
worked with Jon's patrol. Jon
nearly died, too. Covered in rub-
ble and wedged under a truck,
it was only his kicking feet that
alerted a teammate he was still
alive. He was admitted to Walter
Reed Army Medical Center, his
body and spirit broken. Turnbull
writes of his despair and how he
cried out to God with prayers
that He would send one of his
angels to help him. His prayers
were answered.

"I was placed on a liquid
diet, so at any time I could make
a request. I asked for special
treats. I am partial to doughnuts,
which is a commonly known fact
to those closest to me. An angel from my hometown decided

to show her love by sending me five dozen doughnuts from a place called Cops and Doughnuts," Jon wrote in the chapter titled, "Angels, Bagels, and Doughnuts, Oh My!"

Bubba and Ryno recalled that Jon's friend Marcy called Cops & Doughnuts and asked the bakery to send a dozen doughnuts to Jon. They did better than that and shipped out five dozen.

"Those got lost in the mail, so we sent five dozen more and all ten dozen must have arrived at the same time," Bubba said.

Turnbull wrote he was praying in bed in his darker-than-usual room, when he heard a knock at the door. It was nurse Gabby, one of his favorite people.

I motioned to her to enter . . . "Sir, I saw you were awake," she told him. "I was eating one of your doughnuts. I have an extra one. Would you like the extra one?" That question lifted my spirits higher than anything else I could think of. A dough-nut brought just for me!

"Yes, ma'am. That would be delightful," I responded with a huge smile on my face." . . .

"Are you an angel?" She chuckled at that, calling me sweet, and left my room . . .

"[Gabby] showed up in my time of need and helped me overcome something that couldn't have been overcome by medicine. Secondly, she had brought me my favorite food on the planet, so there was that. . . . Closing my eyes to go to sleep, I knew that God had my back and that I was safe with angels constantly surrounding me."

Jon later sent Bubba and Ryno a copy of his memoir, writing, "God bless you!"

Chapter 4

BUILDING A BIG BUSINESS THE SMALL-TOWN WAY

It was August 2009 and a lucky break was brewing. A suspected embezzler had abandoned his carpet store and fled town. The Clare city cops had intended to serve a felony warrant for his arrest, but they weren't overly disappointed. They knew he'd get picked up later, for one. And now they had the chance to buy the abandoned building.

To back up a little, Cops & Doughnuts had enjoyed a great summer—the national media publicity had drawn thousands of new customers. But the tiny bakery had only enough room for two small tables. The cold Michigan winter would soon arrive, and customers would need a warm, spacious place to enjoy their coffee and doughnuts.

As it so happened, the carpet store owner was allegedly embezzling money from customers of Kevin's Carpet, which was located next door to the bakery.

"This guy's business plan was 'give me a 50 percent cash deposit, and you'll never, ever hear from me again,'" Bubba said.

When the carpet store owner heard the police were after him, he loaded up everything of value in the store and skipped town, leaving only carpet scraps in his wake. Ryno heard the news and immediately called down to Florida to ask the building owner if Cops & Doughnuts could buy the store.

"It's available," Bill Barz told him. "I had sold it to Kevin on land contract, no money down, and he never made a single payment."

"Well, he was also ripping off his customers," Ryno informed him. "The guy just fled town and he's going to prison."

The two men agreed on a price for the century-old building—$85,000—and sealed the deal that day with a $5,000 down payment. Ryno asked Barz a bit later if he could knock a hole between the two buildings for a doorway.

"Sure, go ahead," the owner said, not bothered by the fact that nothing was in writing.

Ryno next called the co-owner of the bakery building and was immediately given permission to knock a hole in the bakery wall. But the cop owners didn't own that building either, at least not yet—they were still leasing it.

Ryno also contacted two semi-retired contractors to see if they could do the job. They said sure, but they could do it *only* on that weekend. They started the work first thing on Saturday morning.

"So, I need a permit, and I call the city building inspector on Saturday morning and tell him I don't own either building, but I just got permission from both owners to knock a hole in them and build an archway, and how the contractor can only fix it this weekend. I could bring in the drawings first thing Monday morning."

As he spoke, Ryno glanced over at the contractor, who had already started bashing in the wall with a sledge hammer.

Ignoring the noise, Ryno told Williams that both buildings were structurally sound and that an archway was the most

Dave Williams, the building inspector, speedily approved the new archway.

stable design possible. The inspector thought about it for a minute and agreed.

Ryno was amazed. He persuaded three reasonable people to say "yes" to a historic building change, arguably breaking every rule there was.

By the time Ryno delivered the required paperwork, the wall had been blown out and the brickwork around the arch nearly completed.

And that's how it's gone over the years. The cops would need permission for this and that, and the small-town chips would fall their way. The townspeople and city officials knew the cops from their years of service and trusted them to do the right thing.

"How could you not encourage and support something like this? This idea of Cops & Doughnuts could only happen in small-town America because of the synergy there. Clare was their town, and these cops saw it was in dire straits. We were going through tough times economically, and I just wanted to help them in any way we could, but not just them. *Any* business. It's a great little community," said Ken Hibl, who added that Clare is special to him too. A retired colonel, he took the job as city manager after serving

Ken Hibl, the former Clare city manager, negotiated cops' wishes while maneuvering city rules.

around the world in the U.S. Army. He and his wife could have lived anywhere, but the city manager job and small-town appeal of Clare attracted them.

The first hurdle was resolving conflict-of-interest concerns; more than a few people feared that cops would devote more time to the bakery than patrolling the roads and bringing criminals to justice.

"Perception, for some, can become reality, so we were very cautious," said Mayor Patrick Humphrey. "We didn't want three police cars sitting out in front of the bakery shop for four hours. It was like

Mayor Patrick Humphrey

a major deal for us because we could have gotten ourselves in deep trouble, had it not gone the way we wanted. But yeah, we took a chance and I'm so thankful that we did. I don't think that people who don't live in the city know all the things that these guys do to give back. It's just unbelievable. They're just so civic-minded."

Early on, people commented about the propriety of cops owning a bakery and asked pointed questions of the city government.

"There is always that small minority, and we had some of that. There were comments, but we responded to them," Ken said. "My guidance to the police chief was, 'Hey, we have to be on the up and up, and certainly cops are allowed to take breaks and work at the bakery during their off hours. But please don't let them park our city vehicles in front of the bakery.'"

The cops followed parking orders, but there was nothing to do about visiting police—sometimes cars from up to three different police agencies parked in front of the bakery.

There were critics in 2010, when TV production crews started coming in, filming the cops for various TV shows.

"There were a lot of times when film crews were downtown, right in front of the bakery, and guys in uniform," Dogman said. "When we did that *Small Town, Big Deal* TV show, they were out filming in the road and riding around in patrol cars. I think the older commissioners, who were kind of set in the ways of the '70s and '80s, were having a difficult time understanding that—believe it or not—this is good for the city. They were, 'It's never going to work' and lo and behold, there's *Fox and Friends*, there's *Stars and Stripes*, and this magazine and that magazine."

Added Ryno: "I know there's a commissioner or two

The TV crew of *Small Town, Big Deal* interviews John and Martha Youstra, Clare's "official grandparents."

that we've won over. You can see them sitting in the bakery now."

Fast forward to 2013 and Ken suggested that the city commission offer Bubba and Ryno an early retirement. It made financial sense. The men were the city's two most senior employees and their earnings and vacation days stood at the top of the pay scale.

At the same time, Cops & Doughnuts was bringing thousands of tourists into Clare.

"All of our passion was going into the bakery, and our passion for police work was dwindling," Bubba said. "Not that we were doing bad work, but they knew we had found our passion. They knew if they offered us an early retirement, we would take this to the next level and bring even more people to town. But when you offer early retirement, you have to offer it to everybody. You just can't offer it to two people."

A Conversation Between Brothers

Clare. A warm day just before St. Patrick's Day and Ryno bumps into his older brother, Tim "T.J." Rynearson outside the bakery. Here's a third-party recording of their conversation—well debate—about crossing the line between public and private interests. Tim used to be the chief of the Clare Police Department, and Ryno used to report to him. The recording starts off with a question: Why does Tim oppose the idea of a cop-owned bakery?

TIM: Because they used too many resources of the city's, and I felt that being tax dollars, we shouldn't have a private business.

RYNO: Even though it was not city dollars. It was our own private business, but you know, Tim couldn't see the end result.

TIM: Oh no, I could.

RYNO: The millions of dollars that we bring to town, from one part-time employee of twenty-four hours a week to now. At one point, we had just in Clare alone, fifty employees. All right? You know, our payroll in the one year was $2.3 million, mostly in Clare.

TIM: The [cops] were representing my department. If you're paying city taxes, it should go towards their work, not for them promoting a business. Simple as that. We're police officers. We have higher standards.

RYNO: Tim's kind of like those Wal-Marts we talk about. I remember watching a program where it took like eight or nine years for a Wal-Mart to build in this one city and there were petitions and all that, and people signed the petitions to keep them out. And Wal-Mart bought all those lists. And then after it was opened, 90-some percent of the people who had signed petitions shopped at Wal-Mart. He's so against this. But he's here two times a day, seven days a week.

TIM: Not twice.

RYNO: At least once. This is your second time today.

TIM: It is. It's a beautiful day, but you know, that was just my thoughts, my views. I felt that, it's a wonderful thing. But still they used police officers, city resources to promote a private business that benefited them. They were in here all the time in uniform. They come in here in uniform all the time.

RYNO: I abused it, although we tried to be really good. But that's why they got Bubba and I out of the department as quickly as they could because we were a lot more beneficial to the city retired and doing this. Tim, did you ever go in the Lone Pine restaurant in uniform? You owned it.

TIM: I did. There was a difference, though.

RYNO: Oh, yeah, of course, yeah.

TIM: And, there again, you knew how I was. I wouldn't even cash my check in the patrol car. I wouldn't even drive through. That's right. That's my private business. You can't do private business on company time. That's just what I believe.

> RYNO: There's nothing wrong with it. Fortunately for us, we had a different view. Downtown right now would be a ghost town.
>
> TIM: Not necessarily. You could have done something else, Ryno.
>
> RYNO: Such as?
>
> TIM: Well, you know, you've always wanted to get into prostitution.
>
> And with that, the conversation dissolves into laughter.

The city commission set down new criteria to qualify for a pension: age fifty and twenty-five years of working for the city. Only Bubba and Ryno fit the criteria—almost. Neither man had quite reached twenty-five years of service, so the city dipped into city coffers for the difference and bought them out.

"We needed to cut a couple of positions," Ken explained. "At the same time, Ryno and Bubba wanted to retire. We offered them a deal if they wanted to go."

"The city came out way ahead on this. And the reason is Ryno and I were at the top of the pay scale, the top of everything. . . . It was almost like they retired a couple of cops and got two tourism directors for nothing," Bubba said.

The cops' can-do attitude—right from the beginning—gained the attention of Jim McBryde, who worked with the Michigan Economic Development Corporation at the time. Historically, MEDC subsidized classic old-school economic development—

that is, a "base economy" of manufacturing, agriculture and mining.

"The old adage was if you can make it, mine it, or grow it, that's a base economy," Jim said. "You know, if you have those type of jobs, it really builds a community and then everything else layers on top of that. Your retail is going to come in, your restaurants are going to come in. Businesses like Amazon, which put in a distribution center, are here now."

James "Jim" McBryde, CEO of the Middle Michigan Development Corporation, views Cops & Doughnuts as an economic engine and anchor for Clare.

But the MEDC made an exception to the "make it, mine it, or grow it" rule after the cop owners had convinced Jim that Cops & Doughnuts was worthy of an investment. Its financial award to a marketing firm wasn't that hefty, but it funded the bakery's effort to initially stock Cops Coffee in grocery stores across the country, Ryno said.

Fast forward to 2015, when Cops & Doughnuts and other downtown retailers were awarded $333,852 to help update the facades of seven buildings, including three belonging to the bakery. The award helped transform the downtown from shabby to stately historic, making it worthy of tourist traffic.

"Cops & Doughnuts is not just a doughnut place. It's not just a restaurant. It's not just baked goods. It's a tourist attraction," said Jim, who takes a bird's-eye view of Michigan businesses. "I justified it initially that way, but as we've worked more with them, it's really become an anchor to the downtown, along with the Doherty Hotel. *And* it is a huge tourist attraction with lines out the door."

During the 2020 and 2021 pandemic years, the MMDC also gave a total of $6 million to the bakery and other Michigan retailers—most of them businesses they've never worked with before—as part of the Michigan Small Business Relief, Restart and Survival Grant programs.

Here are a few stories of how a small town went big for cops and doughnuts.

Favors Go Both Ways

In 2010, the Clare Police Department Chief Dwayne "Midge" Miedzianowski (a Cops & Doughnuts cop owner) ruefully mentioned to Ryno that he bought the wrong size of shoulder patches—a waste of $100.

Ryno told the chief, "No problem, the bakery can take them off your hands so you don't lose money."

They bought all 100 patches for the cost of about ninety cents each and sold some of them for $4.95 apiece. But mostly, they traded them with patches brought in by visiting police officers.

Color Blind

In 2009, a week before they opened, Ryno showed the city manager the new Cops & Doughnuts website.

"Why is [Officer] Brian Gregory in a gray shirt instead of a blue shirt?" Ken asked.

"Well, we can't do that. If you look, there's no shoulder patch either, there's no badge or nothing," Ryno said.

He told Ken that they were complying with the city's internal policy: Clare city police could not wear their light-blue uniform, badge or shoulder patch for financial gain. So, to comply, Ryno had photoshopped in gray shirts and positioned Gregory so that his badge and shoulder patch didn't show.

Ken said he was aware of the policy and appreciated Ryno following the rules.

"But you change that gray shirt to blue. We'll get that uniform policy changed straight away."

And he did.

Dressed for Travel

In 2013, four of the cop owners traveled to England to take part in a one-day event, "Policing Through the Ages."

The English cops in South Hampshire and Portsmouth had invited the Clare bakery owners to tour the country dressed in full police uniform. But would that violate the city's internal policy? The city commission met, had a short discussion, and granted permission for the cops to wear their official uniforms.

So, on the day of the event, they arrived in full Clare cop regalia: their light-blue uniform, duty belts and handcuffs. But no sidearms or holsters, per English tradition.

Working the Night Shift

After the first year in operation, an idea was percolating—what if the cops sold private-label Cops & Doughnuts coffee in the bakery and on the website? People could buy it for themselves or as a gift or souvenir.

COPS & DOUGHNUTS

Their first step was to approach their supplier—Paramount Coffee Company, in Lansing, Michigan, an employee-owned company.

Ryno and Bubba proposed the idea to the executive of Paramount Coffee, but were met with resistance. They were told the company already had its hands full packaging private-label coffee for Biggby Coffee, which was expanding like crazy throughout the state. They didn't want to get weighed down with other small companies wanting the same.

Forced to seek out a different company, the cops contacted Ferris Coffee & Nut Company based in Grand Rapids. The executives there warmly welcomed the opportunity and agreed to meet.

A few weeks later, an executive from Ferris Coffee sat with Ryno at the roundtable to finalize the terms. Overhearing the conversation was Elise, one of the bakery's front counter persons. At the time, her husband, Wade, was a Paramount sales rep and one of his biggest accounts was Cops & Doughnuts. She decided she'd better give him a quick call.

"Hey, Wade," she told her husband. "You're about to lose the account here with Cops & Doughnuts, and we are buying a lot of coffee from you. Remember how they wanted to do private-label bags and your guys said no? Well, they've got Ferris Coffee right here in the bakery, and they've agreed to do it for them."

The last-minute plea worked.

The next day Paramount reached out to Ryno, finally agreeing to the private label. Now Cops Coffee is a strong source of revenue for the bakery and for Paramount.

Not so Lucky in a Big Town

Ryno wanted to go big with Cops & Doughnuts coffee, so he called the executives of SpartanNash grocery store chain to get them to agree to "slot" Cops & Doughnuts coffee on their store shelves. But the challenge in the grocery business is shelf space is scarce and you have to pay to play—in this case, $20,000 for each blend.

"Well, we didn't have that kind of money at that time. And when we did have the money and tried to slot one of them, they still said no," Ryno said.

The Clare cops tried their small-town approach. They put a Coffee & Doughnuts ad on the billboard on US 131 just north of SpartanNash headquarters in the much larger city of Grand Rapids. Going one step further, they contacted a local trucking company located next to the SpartanNash offices and bought massive coffee ads to put on their semitrucks. For two years, the executives saw the billboard on their way to work and home, and watched the semitrucks drive back and forth with the Coffee & Doughnuts ads.

And they *still* said no.

"I don't know why," Ryno admitted. "We did everything we could."

Doughnut Ring-In-The-New-Year!

In a small town, you need to create your own fun. It was New Year's Eve and Mayor Humphrey was sitting at the bakery with a few of the police officers. It was getting dark.

"There wasn't much going on that night, so we decided to do our own New Year's countdown," Humphrey said. "Ryno went to the upstairs window, Bubba was downstairs, and they hung a rope from the window to the sidewalk just in front of the bakery. I was standing at the curb with a camera. Ryno took one of these big fluffy cloth doughnuts they have and sent it down the rope, while I did the countdown: ten, nine, eight, seven. . . ."

A Small Town Has Eyes

Small towns can also have its disadvantages, Mayor Humphrey said.

"One day I was at the bakery and I walked across the street to my truck instead of walking to the corner and crossing. My photo ended up the next day on the front page of the paper. I'm the mayor and I set the example for everybody. I mean, you can't be legislating laws and then breaking them yourself. That's just plain common sense."

And, finally, the end of the story of Kevin's Carpets. After the fugitive was found, he was arrested, brought to court and found guilty. He asked the judge if he could be granted a twelve-hour work release, explaining that he had a carpet store to run. The judge consulted with a Clare officer, who reported in due course that the man was lying. The carpet store was now a bakery, owned by nine cops—the same cops who had intended to serve him a felony warrant before he fled town.

The judge laughed—small-town justice at its finest—and dismissed the request.

Chapter 5

THE DISNEY OF THE DOUGHNUT WORLD

On Saturdays at lunchtime in the summer of 2021, Angela Isaac hustled from one table to the next, taking orders and silently cursing the Cops & Doughnuts guys. She says she's joking, but maybe only a little.

"The town was so busy and we were short-staffed," said Angela, a waitress who works at the Timeout Tavern (a 30-second walk from the bakery). "I thought to myself, 'What have you done to our sleepy little town?' We see people walking the sidewalk, carrying white boxes. We call them 'The Doughnut Walkers.'"

What have they done indeed? From June to late August, tourists and summer residents swarm the town. They exit off the expressway to visit Cops & Doughnuts on the main drag and other small-town attractions. Most are on their way to somewhere else: the family cottage, the National Cherry Festival in Traverse City, or Mackinac Island.

Ryno remembers a time when three young women blew into the bakery, yelling, "Yay! We made it! We just drove four hundred miles."

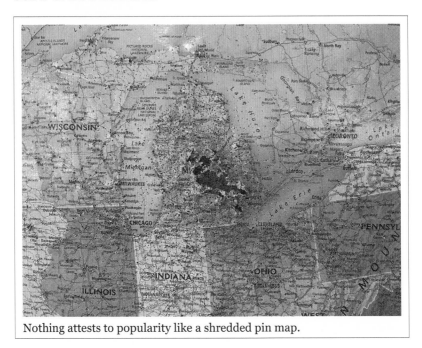

Nothing attests to popularity like a shredded pin map.

In 2018, buses pulled in from Pennsylvania, the Dakotas and Ohio. Many were on "Mystery Tours of Michigan," which takes Indiana and Michigan tourists to surprise destinations. Other buses, returning downstate from Mackinac Island, sometimes stop at Clare for lunch and a doughnut. By the end of the year, Bubba and Ryno tallied a total of more than one hundred buses.

"People come in from every state you can imagine. Prior to COVID, we had people flying in from England. We are world famous," said Ryno, the master of hyperbole. "The buses come during the peak travel time and also October is huge with color tours. And then, COVID killed it in 2020."

Fortunately, he said, the bakery is bouncing right back.

Scenes of the bakery's summer sidewalk at the peak of tourist season.

COPS & DOUGHNUTS

Fortunately, at Cops & Doughnuts, they put the real bathroom locks on the *inside*.

"Last year, 2021, was the first we'd seen buses since COVID hit. Maybe there were five or six," Ryno said. "I'm just really proud we're such an attraction. The buses used to drive by Clare and now they have a reason to come off the expressway."

But, come on, bus tours? To a *bakery*? But Cops & Doughnuts isn't just any bakery.

The cop owners aim to create an "experience." First stop after a long drive is the bathroom. A sign directs visitors to the "Booking Bathroom>>>4U2P" with jail bars and a padlock painted on the door.

Sure to catch your eye, on the way, is the classic photo of a tough-looking young cop wearing sunglasses, holding a radar gun in one hand and a doughnut in another. Linger a bit, and you'll see Bubba's favorite Norman Rockwell painting of a little boy sitting up at a doughnut bar with a cop. Once you get your doughnut, you might sit at the roundtable with cops, but heed the banner: "OLD COOTS GIVING ADVICE: It's probably bad advice, but it's free."

Kids of all ages play cops and robbers.

COPS & DOUGHNUTS

Yesterday's doughnuts are today's parolees.

Lincoln, Renya and Kolten Ricola behind bars.

Step outside to the back alley and get your picture taken in front of one of the eccentric, multicolored murals, including a massive doughnut, filled with . . . doughnut sculptures. Don't miss seeing the sign: "Inmate of the Month: Parking Only." A sign on the exposed walk-in freezer reads, "City Morgue." And back inside, gaze at the thousands of cop shoulder patches from around the world and shirts upon shirts: "YOU HAVE THE RIGHT TO REMAIN GLAZED." "D.W.I. Doughnuts Were Involved," "M, GLAZE AND BLUE," "Don't Glaze me bro."

Or step in front of the bakery and

get your picture taken in the crazy photo stand-in.

Help yourself to a plateful of day-old doughnuts where a sign announces: "Parolees last chance!" Read the framed news articles about a doughnut heist from a convenience store. Get your mug shot taken with Ryno or Bubba, but be prepared to confess to your real height. There is jokey stuff everywhere, making you realize, "Whoa! Cops do have a sense of humor!"

"We come up with these things around a bonfire with a six-pack of beer," said Bubba, disclosing the cops' painstaking marketing plan.

Joshua Lator, the state police commander of the nearby Mount Pleasant post, said his wife's relatives from Arizona consider a bakery stop right up there with the Mackinac Bridge and Tahquamenon Falls.

Mugging for a mug shot.

"They always want to go to Cops & Doughnuts, even though they've been there multiple times. And it's not just the kids, it's the adults too. They want to take some pictures to put on social media, so all their friends back in Arizona see that they got to go to Cops & Doughnuts. Yeah, so the Disney World of the doughnut world, that is legitimate."

"Sometimes the counter staff asks, 'Why do you make such a big deal out of this thing?'" Ryno said.

COPS & DOUGHNUTS

Ryno and Bubba pose with themselves.

"Well, you know what? This is a big deal because we had a family that traveled here one time, a single mom and her son, and her son's friend. They came here on spring break from Wisconsin because she couldn't afford to take him to an amusement park or a beach down south, so they stayed at the Doherty Hotel, and for them, it was a big deal. Dogman said it first: we're an event, not a bakery."

And, of course, doughnuts aren't the main attraction. It's doughnuts *and* cops.

"I always tell the new hires. You're not selling doughnuts. You're selling cops selling doughnuts. There's a big difference," said Bubba, who shouts out a greeting to nearly everyone who steps through the door.

The counter people are called the "Directors of First Impressions."

Bubba admits, humbly, that he and Ryno have become a bit of a draw. People often ask to take their "mug shot" with them.

One day, Bubba and his wife were shopping in nearby Bay City, Michigan, and a family scurried up to him, a little breathless to meet Bubba before he left the store.

"You're Bubba from Cops & Doughnuts, aren't you?" asked the 11-year-old girl.

"Yeah, I am," said Bubba. "Do you like doughnuts?"

"Yeah," she said and paused. "Wow. I've never met a celebrity before."

This was early on and Bubba was taken aback. For the first time, perhaps in his entire life, he was speechless.

Ryno, who drives an aging, un-celebrity-like Mercury Marquis, remembers a young man standing in line for doughnuts, staring at him and Bubba with a deer-in-the-headlights look.

"Well, then he sends a message about an hour later through our Facebook. And he goes, 'Hey, I was in your place today, and I follow you all the time, and I seen Bubba and Ryno. Is it OK if I approach him and talk to them?' And then there was another guy from Texas. He goes, 'You guys here, you're nearly famous.' That's us!"

Eric Stadler and his son stop for doughnuts and drinks while charging their electric car.

COPS & DOUGHNUTS

Parking becomes scarce in the summertime, prompting the cop owners to make a strict rule: employees may not park in front of the bakery or anywhere on the street side, only in the larger municipal lots.

"If anyone gets caught doing it, even an owner, you have to pay a $20 fine and that goes into a jar for charity," Bubba said. "Over the years, we broke that rule for one employee. We had a seventeen-year-old boy working for us. His name was Derek Winter, and he was a good-looking young man. He was always singing at different school events, a lot of times, the national anthem. He was such a heartthrob to all the teen girls, and everybody knew his truck. If he was parked in front of the bakery, we sold a lot of doughnuts when he was here. We told him, 'Anytime you work, you can take a spot in front of the bakery!'"

The reality is, a lot of middle- and low-income families can't afford to visit the expensive land of Disney, so they come to Cops & Doughnuts, knowing they'll have a good time. The cops are proud that they can offer an affordable outing.

"We had something happen here yesterday," Bubba said. "A nice young family—a mom, dad and two boys, around six and eight years old—I got talking to them. They live in the West Branch area, and one of the boys was having a birthday. They'd asked him what he wanted to do, and the only thing he wanted was to go to Cops & Doughnuts. They went out and got lunch, they got doughnuts, took pictures, they were in here for an hour. When we say the Disneyland of Clare, we are thinking it costs a lot of money to take your kids to Disneyland, but it's really reasonable to bring them here. It's a nice outing, and it's special, and I'm proud of that."

Eric Stadler says it's a tradition to visit Cops & Doughnuts with his son, Eric, while he charges his electric car a block away. They're sitting outside in the springtime sun, enjoying doughnuts with Mountain Dew and chocolate milk.

The cops bake up a memorable visit for families, inviting them to take a mug shot or even a bakery tour, depending on the time of day. Bubba likes to tell kids funny stories and pass out stickers to the little ones.

"We need to make it a special experience; we need to make it fun. And that's what we do!" Ryno said.

Speaking of which . . . one day, shortly after the bakery opened, a dad came in with his ten-year-old boy and energetic five-year-old girl. The boy quickly picked out his doughnut, but the little girl paced back and forth in front of the display case, her brow furrowed as she scanned the dozens and dozens of doughnuts.

"Is there a special doughnut you're looking for?" the teen at the counter asked.

"Yeah, I want a doughnut with pink frosting," she said. "But you don't have a doughnut with pink frosting."

"Well, you know what?" said the teenage girl. "I thought you might be coming in today, and I saved one just for you. I'll go get it!"

She walked back to the prep room with Bubba following right behind her. He was curious . . . he knew they didn't make pink-frosted doughnuts. But he watched the girl spoon out some white frosting in a little bowl, add a couple of drops of red food coloring, and whip up some pretty pink frosting. She slathered it onto the doughnut and finished it off with a few sprinkles.

When she brought it out, the little girl lit up like she'd been given a pony. "Thank you soooo much!" she gushed.

The father looked at Bubba like, "I can't believe customer service can be like this!"

A few days later, Ryno and Bubba were sitting out on the sidewalk with the guy who was getting ready to put up the three-dimensional Cops & Doughnuts sign.

"Hey," he said. "What color do you want the frosting?"

"Pink," Bubba said. "Make it pink with sprinkles."

CLARE'S OTHER ATTRACTIONS

The bakery's tourist draw has spread over the rest of Clare like a fast-moving dough boy ever since 2009, when the bakery opened its doors.

"Clare has the Doherty Hotel, the Whitehouse Restaurant, the 500 District, all these great thriving businesses, but when I go to a conference and I say Clare, Michigan, people say, 'Yeah, Cops & Doughnuts. I love their doughnuts. Every time I come up north, I'll stop and get a doughnut and maybe dessert, buy swag from their shop, and then find something to eat at another restaurant,'" said Jeremy Howard, Clare's city manager.

The Whitehouse Restaurant and historic Doherty Hotel were tourist destinations long before Cops & Doughnuts. Doherty is famous for its fine dining and 157 fancy hotel rooms. An elegant hotel, it's the site of the not-so-elegant murder of Isaiah Leebove in 1938. A wealthy oil man and attorney, Leebove moved to the sleepy town of Clare after getting into trouble with the law. Living on the outskirts of Clare, he built a mansion and an expansive game retreat for his rich hunting buddies to enjoy. It was a nice life until his relationship with the Purple Gang ultimately led to his paranoid business partner shooting him to death on a May evening.

There's entrepreneur Morgan Humphrey, who has created another Clare attraction: District 500. It's a sprawling, three-story building that caters to every human desire: delicious food, a yen for an evening cocktail, and couples who want to get married.

Jeremy Howard, Clare city manager

Morgan, who looks more like a fashion model than a business owner, has created an ambitious enterprise. It all started with the 505 Café, which she opened at the age of nineteen. She expanded to a wedding venue on the second floor and added elegant bedroom and bathroom suites on the third floor—an all-in-one bridal paradise, where the bridal party can spend the night and get gussied up the next day before a bank of mirrors and blow dryers. As a final touch, she added The Trap Door in the basement, a speakeasy-style bar, that's often packed wall-to-wall with folks seeking company in the lonely months of winter.

Morgan has taken advantage of the popularity of destination weddings. She noted that Clare is now in the running with Hawaii, Greece and the California shoreline. Some people—maybe seeking a break from a high-stress world—come to Clare, Michigan, to experience small-town life.

Morgan Humphrey has created a downtown empire of her own.

"We are a destination player. We've got a wedding party coming in from Canada this next weekend," Morgan said, as her staff scurried around getting ready for St. Patrick's Day, which draws 10,000 people every year.

"The only thing you have to worry about in Clare is an Amish buggy going too slow or something, and, yeah, the horse doo."

And speaking of doo, there is a lot to *do* in Clare: golfing, downhill and cross-country skiing, biking, hunting, gambling (in Mt. Pleasant), hunting, fishing, the St. Patrick's Day parade . . . even cruising down a zip line! What you won't find are traffic jams or parking meters. Yes!

The Amish community attracts thousands to Clare every spring and fall with its large quilt auction, craft show, and flea market. Hundreds of vendors set up their wares in fields: arts and crafts, jewelry, tools, jams, plants, cheese, baked goods, and much more. During the rest of the year, people are invited to take a self-guided tour of small Amish retailers.

Finally, tourists visit Calla Lily, a boutique right next door to the bakery. Owner Lacey Badelt is often the star of Cops & Doughnuts social media posts. Bubba and Ryno sometimes don her clothing to hilarious effect. In fact, besides her husband, Bubba and Ryno are her strongest supporters.

"From the day I opened, it was like, 'Go, go, go! You can do this! We're right next door. You can handle it. You can do anything you want!'"

And they should know.

Chapter 6

REALITY TV THAT NEVER GOT REAL

It was close to midnight when Ryno was driving his patrol car down Main Street and saw a woman perched on the back of an overgrown rooster—a fiberglass sculpture in front of The Evening Post Bar & Grill, a popular restaurant. Acting like she had five beers too many, she howled obscenities in the cool March air. Ryno switched on his emergency lights and pulled over to check things out.

The woman was Jennifer Tisdale, sister of Ashley Tisdale, both gorgeous, 20-something actors who run Blondie Girl Productions. She was visiting Clare for a few days to make a sizzle reel for a proposed reality TV show of Cops & Doughnuts. They'd planned to shop it around to networks with hopes of getting funding for an entire season of six episodes. (Funding for the sizzle reel came from Food Network.)

The scripted scene was inspired by an odd practice in Clare of young women getting plastered after drinking all night and climbing onto the rooster, singing and yelling words young children shouldn't hear.

Ryno—who was new to acting and actually on duty—stepped out of his patrol car and ordered Jennifer to get off the rooster. She refused. He had no option but to climb up and wrap his arms around her and slide down the side of the rooster. In multiple takes, he tried different ways to get her down, including Jennifer sliding down into his waiting arms. All this action was a little too up close and embarrassing for Ryno, but Jennifer assured him she was a professional.

Once Jennifer was firmly back on the sidewalk, Ryno told her she was too drunk to drive and to call someone for a ride home. He walked her down the block to Cops & Doughnuts, where studio lights and a TV camera awaited her entry. Moments later, Lt. Greg "Bulldog" Kolhoff—a gruff-looking ex-marine in real life—walked into the bakery and the two sat down in front of the window for a little talk, a camera capturing the scene from the outside sidewalk.

Randy Hale prepping Ryno for a sizzle reel traffic stop.

COPS & DOUGHNUTS

After chatting for a few minutes, Jennifer, still in character as a sloppy drunk, couldn't hold her coffee and doughnuts, and spat a dark slurry into Bulldog's face. Fortunately, the spitting scene took only two takes.

During the next several days, the cops were at the beck and call of Jennifer and Jonathan Karsh, the tall, thin cameraman, finding extras, props and locations.

This was in 2013, ostensibly before Blondie Girl Productions specialized in TV shows made by and for millennial women. The nine cops were definitely *not* that. But the intended show aimed to capture the "reality" of small-town cops running a bakery while bringing ne'er-do-wells to justice.

The cops wouldn't get paid if the show got the green light, but Ryno liked the idea of free national publicity—good for the bakery, good for Clare.

Jennifer and Karsh had flown in from Los Angeles with three days of "reality" scripts in hand. And for Ryno, that was revelation No. 1: "reality" TV is about as far from reality as doughnuts are from green cabbage. It's completely scripted.

The cops were actually on duty during the filming and getting paid. Explained Ryno: "We went to the city commission to get permission to do the show. We said, 'We hope you say yes because the production crew is already on their way to Clare.' They didn't vote yes, but they didn't vote no, either."

As the filming wrapped up and just before Jennifer and Karsh flew back to Los Angeles, they promised the cops they would give them a sizzle reel even if the reality TV show never got made. And that's where the unhappy ending began to unwind.

A local prosecutor thought of the ramifications of Jennifer and the production crew witnessing an actual criminal action or an arrest gone wrong. If the case ever came to trial, Tisdale (or any other crew member) might be required to appear in court as a witness.

"She stood firm and told them that's the way it's going to be. There was a little bit of discussion. When they finished filming and everything was done, there was a slight conversation, but there wasn't any heart in trying to negotiate," Ryno said.

"We were really disappointed, given the fact there are all kinds of ride-around-with-cops shows that don't do that," Bubba said. "Just for example, if they're out riding with Officer Kolhoff and he pulls over a drunk driver and the man or woman pleads not guilty and demands a trial, anyone on the film crew would be subject to a subpoena because they were witness to the sobriety test and arrest. For a minor crime like that, I don't think it's really necessary. If there was a shooting or something, yeah, you would need them as an eyewitness. I think the prosecutor truly felt this was the right decision and didn't intend to throw a wrench in the show."

But the prospect of getting called into court to testify, anywhere at any time, got a hard "no" from the Blondie Girls. Ryno never heard from the Tisdale sisters again. He didn't get a sizzle reel either.

When Ryno got a second call to

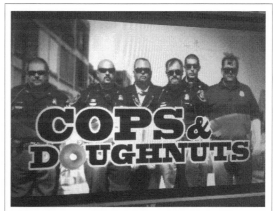

The cops never got a sizzle reel, but they did get this one photo.

explore a reality show a few months later, he explained what had happened with the first. But that didn't seem to deter PSG Films, which had hired Lee Christofferson and Stan McMeekin, an Emmy-award winning cameraman and producer, an additional camera gal, and a soundman.

This time the cops decided to invest more energy into the effort and put in fourteen-hour days. They promised the crew they would deliver *anything* they needed.

"We can get anything. When you're a cop in a small town, you know everybody. I can get you anything you want," Bubba told him.

McMeekin took them at their word and asked for a plane . . . that very afternoon.

"He said it would be really cool—this was back before drones—to take an aerial shot of a cop pulling over a car," Ryno said.

Ryno called Ron Kunse, a local developer and pilot (Ryno kiddingly calls him "Airplane Driver"), and he agreed to get

Pilot Ron Kunse with Lee Christofferson (behind the camera) and Stan McMeekin.

his plane revved up and ready to go within an hour. No liability forms, no insurance, no payment to Kunse, not even for gas. Just a handshake and a thank you.

On another midnight shoot, the cameraman was going to ride with Bubba; he was working third shift that night. Wanting to make a good impression, Bubba decided to give the car a late-night wash.

"I took it down to the car wash and sprayed it off really good. I didn't want a bunch of water spots, so I did something that cops do. I took it to the freeway and drove it 100 miles an hour to dry it off. Then a deer jumps out in front of me and smashed the car, and it did a lot of damage."

Fortunately, Bubba was unhurt and the police car, nearly new, wasn't totaled.

"The faster you hit 'em, the quicker they fly off," Bubba said, explaining the physics of car-deer encounters.

Bubba also credited the patrol car's push bumper, a device installed in front of the bumper and made of welded steel—perfect for fending off deer collisions and pushing cars out of snow without leaving a dent.

Bubba showed up at the bakery and casually explained what had happened. He apologized for needing to delay the shoot a little, but he had to go back to the cop shop to file a report and pick up a new car.

Lee was stunned. *Driving at 100 miles per hour to dry off a car?*

"She was stunned by everything," Bubba said. "She was from Seattle, and this was all new to her. She had never seen police like us—so easygoing, so small-town." And so well-connected.

COPS & DOUGHNUTS

When Lee wanted to recreate the lineup of the bakery's opening day, Ryno posted a shout-out on Facebook at 3 p.m.: "Tomorrow morning, we need a line around the corner at 8:45 a.m., and we're filming at 9 a.m. Everyone in line gets a free coffee and a doughnut."

Extras lined up around the corner.

The next morning, a line of more than 100 people snaked around the corner. One teacher brought her entire class down to join in.

"That was a lot of fun, filming it," Ryno said.

There were some artistic differences, i.e., the Clare cops didn't want to be portrayed slamming suspects into the ground or shouting obscenities at each other. In one scene, Dogman was shooting holes in jeans that didn't sell at a local store (more on that in the "From Cool Ideas to Clunkers" chapter).

"They had us argue about it, but they thought we were too mild. It was dumb and stupid. We didn't want the made-up stuff. We told them, we want this to be a modern-day Andy Griffith show. Real life in the bakery and real life on the street," Ryno said.

"They wanted it more edgy," Bubba added, "and that's just not us. We're actually pretty nice guys and the town is really friendly. The other thing they wanted was drama between our wives, a

Emmy award-winner Stan McMeekin pictured on the roof of the Doherty Hotel with his second cameraperson.

situation where two of the wives don't like each other. A drama here, a drama there. That's not the direction we wanted to go."

Revelation No. 2—Reality TV wants edgy, but Clare just isn't. Not the people, not the crimes.

"I span thirty years working here," Bubba said. "We've never had a bank robbery, and we've had a homicide once about every ten years. Two were women who killed their boyfriends, and one, a guy who killed his girlfriend. The number one crime is theft from an auto, kids who go around and try car doors and steal anything they can."

Most recently in the spring of 2022, a Clare man killed an intruder who had broken into his house.

Even meth production was never a problem within the city limits because of the telltale odor. Meth labs once abounded in rural areas, but cheaper drug imports from Mexico priced them out of the market.

The third attempt at a reality show came in 2015 when Ian Sambor, a producer of *Shark Tank*, came to town. He had heard about Clare from a dog trainer who appeared on *Shark Tank* to promote his dog training business for personal security. He had told Sambor about meeting Brian "Dogman" Gregory, the Clare police K9 dog trainer, and learning about the nine cops buying the bakery.

"Ian was a producer for *Shark Tank*, but in the off-season he would do other stuff," Bubba said, "so he reached out to us, and said 'I think there might be a show there. I'd like to spend a few days with you.'"

Unlike the first two producers, he didn't do any filming, but hung around with the cops a few days to see if there might be a show.

"He was born and raised in New York City and went to college in New York. His first job was in Los Angeles, so he had no idea of what small-town America was about," Bubba said. "He said after the second day, 'Is this real?' It made me think of the movie *Funny Farm* with Chevy Chase where they paid the whole town to act normal. Ian honestly thought that we went around and told everybody we have this producer from California coming in, so everybody be cool. He couldn't believe how nice everybody was."

Sambor left, unconvinced he could make a reality TV show. The town was *too* friendly, not to mention the risk of getting a subpoena to testify in court.

There were other attempts, too. In 2016, Original Media reached out and the producer did a ton of interviews over

Skype, including with the three "Bakery Babes"—wives of the principal cops: Tammy (Ryno), Nettie (Bubba) and Denise (Dog-man). The last the cops heard, Bryan Severence, the vice president of development, said he was still working on selling the show.

A year later, Ryno did lots of paperwork to set the stage for Machete Productions, creators of *The Profit* TV show. He emailed them several times and has heard nothing since July 2021.

But wait! There's more! In 2021, Zoran Zgonc reached out on behalf of Magilla Entertainment, a New York City-based production company with shows on such networks as Discovery Channel, History Channel, HGTV, and more.

"We are currently developing series and specials for our network clients, and I'd love to speak more with you about your impressive business, and our proven track record," Zoran wrote.

Ryno took this last communique in stride. It's like anything: the first time is exhilarating, and after a number of years and so many dead ends—not so much.

"We'll do what they want, and if it happens, that's great," Ryno said. "But it's like anything. In the beginning you're gung-ho, but after you've done it a few times, it's more like 'been there, done that, let's just get 'er done.'"

Chapter 7

SERVING UP COFFEE IN JOLLY OLD ENGLAND

Cops & Doughnuts isn't an international brand . . . yet. But the bakery's specialty Cops Coffee made a splash overseas back in 2013, when four cops attended a festival in England called Policing Through the Ages.

The one-day event in early October drew a record 42,000 people, including 3,400 lucky attendees who picked up a free bag of Cops & Doughnuts Cops Coffee.

"This was such a big event. Who'd have thought a little bakery in Clare would be over in England at an international policing event?" said Dogman.

The traveling Clare cop owners included Dogman with his girlfriend (and now wife) Denise; Beaver; police Captain David "Grasshopper" Saad; and Ryno and his wife, Tammy.

In 2013, the bakery was rocking and rolling, the coffee was trademarked, and Ryno was promoting the Morning Shift, Midnight Shift and Off-Duty Decaf blends to stores across the country.

"My thought behind investing $12,500 in the trip was to help Cops Coffee take off nationally. We wanted people to know we really are this big deal."

It all started with a tweet in 2010, a year after the bakery opened.

"I was traveling around the country pushing our Cops & Doughnuts Cops Coffee. We could get it into stores, but I wasn't able to get it slotted into warehouses, which meant the stores couldn't reorder easily and keep it on the shelves," Ryno said.

"Anyway, to promote it, I did a hashtag for copscoffee— that's when hashtags were new—and I found out that the Hampshire police in Portsmouth use the same hash tag. What it meant for them was to meet back at the police station for a coffee break."

So started a friendship with Sergeant Rob Sutton, who told Ryno about the upcoming Policing Through the Ages festival scheduled for October of 2010. Ryno couldn't attend, but he shipped over a few Cops & Doughnuts T-shirts and bags of Cops Coffee for Sutton to pass out to festivalgoers.

Surprise! These English cops were coffee people, too—not necessarily tea!

And just like so many other U.S. police stations, the Portsmouth police (part of the Hampshire Constabulary) were seeking to build better relationships with their community. In fact, that's why they created the festival, Ryno said.

"I learned that the locals treat the police like crap. On the other hand, visitors who come to England love cops, so they were trying to soften up the community with this event. That was key."

Fast forward to 2012, Sutton invited Ryno to their second Policing Through the Ages festival on October 5, 2013.

Ryno looked ahead—by then he'd be fifty and retiring from the police force to run Cops & Doughnuts full-time. Perfect timing!

COPS & DOUGHNUTS

Cops & Doughnuts Chaplain Jim Walter saying a prayer for the travelers before they left for the airport.

Yet he'd *never* flown on a commercial flight, not to mention an overseas flight. When the day finally came, he was nervous. Fortunately, his wife, Tammy, could show him the ropes of baggage claims, boarding passes, gates, and rules about carrying guns. Ryno decided to leave his concealed gun at home, as did the other three cops who were joining him on the trip.

The troupe was supposed to leave from Flint's Bishop Airport, but weather in Chicago delayed the flight, so the airline found an available flight on a different airline leaving Detroit. The troupe was hustled into a van, which sped off to Detroit Metro Airport.

Even so, they barely made it onto the plane. In fact, an airline attendant was holding the door when they arrived.

"It was crazy, but we got there," added Dogman.

The free coffee samples arrived in England a few weeks before the cops did. Sergeant Sutton and his buddy picked up the boxes—3,000 bags of the one-pot packs and 400 twelve-ounce display bags. The rules of shipment were complicated, so much so that Ryno had to first find and pay a customs broker $450 plus shipping costs just to make it happen.

After landing, the cops drove two hours from London Heathrow Airport to Portsmouth, an island city on the southern tip of England. Beaver had reserved what was called a full-sized van, but "a full-size van is like a minivan for us." Their suitcases were packed tight with people sitting on the floor. Beaver got an instant lesson on driving on the left side of the road.

"We had an instance of going around a funky curve and ended up going against incoming traffic. That was the only time. Everyone was hollering and screaming at once," Beaver said.

The festival was held at Gunwharf Quays, a sprawling outdoor shopping center of more than ninety shops. Just across the street, Lady Gaga could gaze on festivities from her top-floor apartment. "I only know that because the Portsmouth cops told me," Ryno said.

The mall is built on a former military site, Gunwharf, where cannons and ammunition were once readied for battle on land and sea. Although many of the structures were destroyed in World War II, some of the 18th and 19th century buildings are still standing and in use.

"The thing that shocked me is they have farm tractors that belong to the police department for rescue. They're a funky blue and yellow with a police department logo," Ryno said.

When the cops arrived in Portsmouth, they were treated like celebrities.

In fact, the Clare cops led the parade of patrol cars driving into the festival in style, cruising in a perfect replica of a Clare Police Department cop car.

COPS & DOUGHNUTS

Cops & Doughnuts . . . leading the parade at Portsmouth!

That patrol car is a story in itself. A couple of months earlier, articles hit the English press about the Clare cops' upcoming trip to Portsmouth. A man by the name of Lindsay Groves reached out to Ryno and made him an offer he couldn't refuse.

"I own a company out here, and I buy police cars and taxis for commercials and films that are made in London. I have a Crown Victoria police car here and could make a replica of your patrol car. You could use it while you're here."

Ryno enthusiastically agreed, promptly secured permission from the Clare City Commission, and sent Groves several photos of the car that he and Bubba drove in together.

The replica was perfect—the only differences were the unit number, the license plates, and a Cops & Doughnuts logo replacing the Clare Police logo.

Following the parade, Beaver drove over to an old building, where several festival volunteers had already set up the Cops & Doughnuts display table, which offered up thousands of free coffee samples. The volunteers explained that the cops' job was to meet and greet visitors, while they manned the table and passed out coffee.

Ryno scanned the rows and rows of displays of different police agencies in the area and the vast number of stores.

In the pier where boats moor, he saw a huge mural: "Policing Through the Ages, Featuring Cops from Michigan USA" with a logo of Cops & Doughnuts. He saw remnants of the military days; the slips where the wooden ships used to come in and big metal rods that would drop the hulls into the harbor of the English Channel.

The Clare cops talked to the English cops and were immediately struck by their language differences.

"We learned new words," Ryno said. "Bobbies don't like to be called bobbies. It's like us being called pigs."

And they learned that England's approach to policing is worlds apart from the U.S.

"Even though we're on the same planet, we police in totally different ways," Dogman said. "They are more technology oriented, and they don't deal with nearly the level of violent crime that we do."

BEATLES, BUCKINGHAM, BUT NO BALLISTICS

The biggest difference between the two countries' approach to crime: most U.K. cops don't carry a gun and residents don't either. A citizen can own a long gun, but it's difficult to get the required permit. Long guns are kept at hunt clubs, not homes, and locked in vaults, Ryno said.

"The police didn't carry guns when we were there. Rob Sutton, the sergeant, only carried a collapsible baton and pepper spray," Ryno said.

COPS & DOUGHNUTS

On a normal shift in Portsmouth, there are forty-one officers on duty. Of those, only four are armed, two to a car. They make up the force's two rapid response units and arrive at a crime scene at the same time as unarmed officers. But what the English police lack in weaponry, they make up with intense surveillance.

"In Gunwharf Quays, they have cameras at every bridge, every tunnel that leads into the island," Ryno said. "They watch every person, every vehicle, every license plate, and they scan every one of our cell phones. As cars entered there, they knew exactly how many people were at the event—42,000—and they knew it for a fact, because there's cameras on every person. They know when you enter the area, and when you leave the area. They even know if someone is listed with INTERPOL [International Criminal Police Organization, the world's largest police organization]."

The surveillance makes the job of policing easier. For example, even as cops are driving to the scene of a crime, they're getting intel on what to expect when they arrive.

"Let's say there are two guys fighting outside a pub," Ryno said. "Before the patrol car ever gets there, the dispatcher is telling him, 'Look out for the guy in a blue shirt, he seems to be the main aggressor, and he just punched the guy in the red shirt.'"

Although this "Big Brother" approach would raise the hackles of some, it doesn't bother Ryno. He believes that cell phones and the Internet have made privacy an illusion.

"It is what it is. If you truly want to get away from everybody, don't take an electronic device because everywhere you go, there's digital trail cams. If you turn your privacy function off on your phone, it just makes it more inconvenient for you. You're still getting tracked. Law enforcement uses satellites and doesn't need a cell tower."

Beaver, Grasshopper, Dogman and Ryno pose in front of the Cops & Doughnuts festival booth.

It was a crisp fall day, perfect weather for a festival. People swarmed the Cops & Doughnuts booth, some wanting to hear their strange American accents and others asking them how cops came to own a bakery. Others wanted to talk to them about the police shows they watched on TV.

COPS & DOUGHNUTS

The English team helps man the Cops & Doughnuts sample table.

"The kids were really the big thing . . . we did a lot of pictures with them," Beaver said. "They watch a lot of American police shows over there, so actually meeting real cops was kind of cool for them."

During the day, the four cops would switch off manning the booth so they could walk around the festival.

"It was amazing, the number of police car collectors over there," said Beaver, who wandered the festival with Grasshopper. "There were so many of them. They're a pretty cool group of people; they get ideas about us by watching TV. There was a Hill Street Blues car and the owner was dressed up like that. Another guy had a Starsky and Hutch car from the old TV show. There were probably twenty American cars."

Dogman and Ryno were walking around when a young woman started hollering at them.

"Mr. Rynearson! Hello, Mr. Rynearson!"

"This is unique, someone knows me all the way across the pond," Ryno thought.

Dogman turned to them and said, "Who did you pay to do that?"

Ryno laughed and said hello to Ms. Maxwell, a girl from Clare whom he barely remembered.

"I read in the paper that you were going to be here, so my husband and I took the train to come and meet you," she said. "I brought this," handing him a box of Krispy Kreme doughnuts.

They all laughed.

After a long day, the four cops walked to their hotel. The next day, they planned an eight-hour driving and walking tour of London. Their favorite moment was walking across Abbey Road just like the Beatles did in their famous picture. "Fifty years ago, four Brits came to the USA. Today, four Americans came to the UK," Ryno pronounced.

Dogman was impressed by the historic remains throughout the city.

"Compared to our country, two hundred and some years old, England has an ancient history that's basically still alive over there—it's amazing. Some of the pubs that we went into were hundreds of years old."

When people saw the patrol car, they'd gather around, thinking they were filming a movie.

Their last stop was Buckingham Palace, where they parked the patrol car in the back.

COPS & DOUGHNUTS

Ryno with an understanding British sergeant.

A big, stern-looking officer approached them.

"Hey guys, what's up?" he said.

"We're just over here from the United States touring around," Ryno said.

"Well, I'm security for the palace, and my sergeant wants to see you around at the West Gate."

The cops looked at each other. "What now?"

Following orders, they drove around to the gate and met the sergeant in charge. He asked them questions, they gave answers. They explained the trip, the patrol car, and their wish

Tourists turn their eyes away from Buckingham Palace to the beauty of a replica Clare cop car.

to get photos in front of the palace. Finally satisfied, he smiled and invited them to park anywhere they wanted, but to stay off the grass. And he promised to mail to them some English cop memorabilia.

As a thank you, Ryno, who had just retired, pulled out his wallet and his badge of thirty years of service. He spontaneously gifted it to him and they bid adieu.

The cops hopped into their patrol car, and parked it in front of Buckingham Palace. As they posed for photos, tourists gathered around to take photos, too, and asked for autographs.

The cops left Cops Coffee samples everywhere they went, including this phone booth.

The cops did *not* meet the queen, however. They were told that a certain flag flies whenever the queen is inside the palace. Today was not that day.

"If she were there, I am sure she would have came right out," Ryno said.

The investment of $12,500 for the trip never paid off. Not a single British order for coffee ever came in. Perhaps it's because the English don't actually like freshly brewed coffee, Beaver said.

"They love their instant coffee," Beaver said. "They like tea, so just like tea, they pour hot water on instant coffee and make coffee that way. Really weird. In fact, we had to give instructions at the festival how to make it."

COPS & DOUGHNUTS

But for years afterward, several of their new English friends would stop at the bakery to say hello, including Lindsay Groves and his wife, Pam.

"Another thing that came out of it—they were inspired by Cops & Doughnuts," Ryno said. "They put a sign on the entrance of the police department—Cops 'n' Coffee. Their door was open two hours on Tuesday and two hours on Saturday. They would have coffee brewed up, and it was a way for people to come in and talk."

And it was inspired by the cops of Michigan USA.

Chapter 8

REAL COPS, REAL DOUGHNUTS, REAL COFFEE

From day one, the doughnuts at Cops & Doughnuts were truly homemade with no preservatives. Preservatives are chemicals, which the Clare cops decided to outlaw from day one. To this day, their doughnuts are made with a mix and ingredients that you can easily pronounce: flour, sugar, yeast, water, eggs. And no sugar-free chemicals either.

"The less chemicals the better," said Ryno. "Dollars-and-cents wise, it *would* make sense to use a preservative. There's a party store chain in Lansing that switched, but it changed the quality and taste of the doughnut. They can send it out to stores for a three-day shelf life, but now their doughnuts are just not as moist or fresh. You can tell you're biting into something like a grocery store product. It's not that bad. They're just drier and kind of blah."

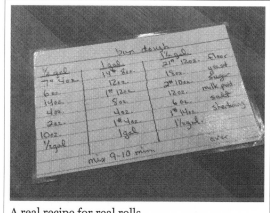

A real recipe for real rolls.

COPS & DOUGHNUTS

This means that the bakery's doughnuts are best eaten within twenty-four hours of getting made. The cops *do* sell day-olds in the store, which still taste pretty delicious. They call them "parolees."

"It's their last chance, either they make it out or they don't," said Bubba, without cracking a smile.

Without preservatives, people are advised to eat their fresh loaf or doughnut right away or freeze it. Otherwise, mold will make an appearance, never a pleasant sight. But it's a learning curve for customers who are used to the preservative-infused bread, like an elderly woman, who carried her molded loaf into the bakery to complain.

"Look at this loaf of bread, I bought it four days ago, and look at all that mold."

"Yes," Ryno said. "Isn't that great?"

"What do you mean, 'Isn't that great?'"

"It means we're not using preservatives. There's no preservatives if it's molded. Try that with Schafer's or Wonder Bread."

Ryno gave her a replacement loaf and a smile, advising her to eat this one more quickly.

"And don't put your bread in the refrigerator either," he said. "You'll just end up with a dry loaf of bread that doesn't taste any good."

The Cops & Doughnuts bakery is somewhat automated, but a far cry from a Wonder Bread factory with an output of 150 loaves *per minute*.

"We have a lot of people working in the back," Ryno said. "There are things we could do to automate, but you don't save any people. You would still need mechanics to run and take care of the equipment. We do use a hopper that injects fillings into two doughnut shells at a time. We fill the doughnuts first and frost them second. Anything that gets glazed gets glazed right out of the fryer, and then they're covered with beautiful sweet love," said Ryno, in an uncharacteristically sentimental moment.

"Even back in the day, they used a cookie cutter. But most of our cookies, jumbo cookies, five ounces, they're hand scooped, like ice cream. For the holidays, we cut them out by hand. We could automate that, but then again, if

Baker Gary Gutzman rocks the rolls.

you replace people who do it by hand, you need maintenance people to take care of the machines. We're all about making jobs for people. It's just tough to hire people in the climate right now."

Bakery manager Sherry Kleinhardt oversees the whole shebang. The recipes have changed over the years—a couple came with the bakery, like the tried-and-true oatmeal cookies.

"There are always ways to improve on stuff—fresher

Bakery manager Sherry Kleinhardt, better known as master of the bakery.

tasting, longer, to make the recipe more economical, some-times you can't get the ingredients anymore. But the doughnut recipes? They're always the same."

Sherry has a big staff to wrangle, ranging from twenty-five in the deep of winter to fifty employees in the tourist-heavy summer. Except for the "Speed Bump" years, she's worked in-credible hours at the bakery, beginning with a straight 180-day stint when the bakery first opened.

Since doughnuts have such a short shelf life, Sherry has to accurately estimate just how many doughnuts—from long johns to Bismarcks to raised and cake—to make each day. Each morning, she starts her guesstimate for the next day of sales. Pencil in hand and filling out column after column, she's guided by experience, intuition, the weather forecast, and time of year.

"It's very hard to read people's minds to know how many customers are going to come in that day. You don't want to run out because then you upset people. You have too much and then there's waste and it's too costly to the business," she said. "So, I mean, there's a lot of factors, like weather events in the area. Gut feeling. Experience. I know, for example, that if it rained yesterday, and the sun's out the next, more people tend to come out. Things like that. I take all those things into consideration with my numbers."

Once the tallies are in place, the doughnut makers start mixing dough at noon. The doughnuts need to be done by 11 p.m. in order to get loaded onto delivery trucks and driv-en to the substations and precincts. The drivers arrive by 4 or 5 a.m., just in time for the morning doughnut seekers.

The frost-and-fill staff arrive at Cops & Doughnuts at 7:00 p.m. and work until three in the morning. When 4 a.m. rolls around,

Nate Pyle (foreground) and
Logan Spicer make doughnuts
for St. Patrick's Day, one of the
busiest days of the year.

Sharon Rissler fills homemade
cream horns.

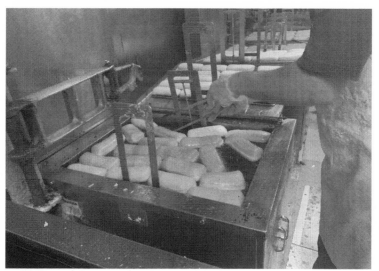

Real doughnuts, really hot.

the pastry staff (usually young women) arrive to make bars, muffins, cookies, and quick breads. Fun fact: doughnuts are the bakery's most popular product, chalking up 80 percent of their baked goods. Cookies, bread, and other treats make up the rest.

Sherry also oversees the baking of up to 200 loaves of bread and nearly 75 dozen buns almost every day, a completely different operation. The bakery's most popular loaf (at least when it comes to website sales) is called salt-rising bread. And that's a surprising fact since its fragrance is kind of funky, smelling a bit like Parmesan cheese. It's a specialty bread made by only a few bakeries in the country.

"Our salt-rising bread is our number one item that we ship out across the country because there's hardly anyone left that makes it," Bubba said. "There's only like three bakeries in the whole United States, as far as I know. And there's only two that ship it out."

Salt-rising bread originated in Appalachia in the 1800s, when yeast wasn't so easy to come by. Like sourdough bread, it grabs wild bacteria from the air. Unlike sourdough bread (which does just fine at room temperature), the starter for salt-rising bread needs a higher heat—but not too high—for the bacteria to grow.

When the cops first took over the bakery, they could buy a ready-made starter, but their supplier went out of business early on. That meant Sherry had to figure out how to make the bread commercially, and it was no easy chore.

Salt-rising bread is made with not one, but two different starters, the first with scalded milk, yellow cornmeal and sugar. The second starter calls for hot water, salt, baking soda, sugar and flour. The starter is particularly fussy and needs constant low heat to grow. In the early days, the baker would set her starter right next to a woodstove. In today's world, the baker can "preheat" the oven with an oven light for two hours, turn it off, and place the loaf inside for eight hours.

You'll know your first starter is on the right track if it smells like your high school son waved his sweaty socks beneath your nostrils. That said, it's not always easy to get the starters to ferment and recipes often mention the prospect of failure.

The bread, in fact, is so fussy that bakers at Cops & Doughnuts had to call their suppliers when the starter wasn't growing normally. It turns out that the cornmeal supplier had changed its blades (to grind the organic cornmeal) and used an anti-bacterial cleaner, which Sherry guessed was killing the wild bacteria.

Despite its funky-smell reputation, salt-rising bread actually tastes better than normal yeast bread. At least that's what Ryno says.

"It toasts right up and you slather it with real butter. I could eat half a loaf with no problem. It's an acquired taste, but some people don't give it a chance because of the stink. Each batch is different, the stinkiness is different. But it seems like the stinkier we can make it, the better people like it. I wish we could buy stink and drop it in. I did find one edible stink, though. But it smelled like poop."

And poop was just going one odor too far. Even for Ryno.

SIP AND SAVOR

The cops are just as proud of their coffee as their bread and doughnuts. Several cop owners went down to Paramount Coffee Company in Lansing for a tour and to create coffee blends they could call their very own.

"Our blends are unique to us," Bubba said. "What they did was they had hired an actual coffee guru. This guy was an Ecuadorian, and he was their coffee expert."

COPS & DOUGHNUTS

The cops were invited to a private table and shown different coffees from all over the world and how they go about creating blends.

"They grind it course, and they put it in a cup of boiling water, and this coffee guru cups his hands around it. And smells it. And then he gets a spoonful and slurps it off the spoon, sucking air with it. He has a different spoon for each blend. They call it a 'cupping slurp.' It's like they have these expert wine tasters, but it's coffee," Ryno said.

The cops sniffed and sipped their way to perfection. Dogman was the coffee connoisseur of the bunch and chose the Night Shift blend (the name has since switched to Midnight Shift). They also created blends for the Morning Shift (light blend) and Off-Duty Decaf. The coffee is a big hit for customers looking for a souvenir or an affordable gift.

THE FISH AND LOAVES DILEMMA

Back in the early days, the cops had a problem. Customers loved the doughnuts, but they kept asking about where to get "real food." As if doughnuts weren't real!

The cops had bought another storefront next to the bakery, giving them extra room, so they opened the Traffic Stop Diner in the spring of 2012. It carried the tagline: "There's nothing routine about our food."

You might recognize the words from news reports: "It was a *routine* traffic stop." Bubba said police get their hackles up when they hear that. Pulling over a car happens to be one of the most dangerous parts of their jobs.

But back to the diner food. It was delicious and truly homemade—perhaps the reason it barely broke even (if that). The

112

The sign for the Pulled Pork Traffic Stop Diner.

cop owners called the café a "loss leader." Sherry called it "foolish."

The café's most popular item was the Double-Up Reuben Sandwich—"double up" is a term that describes two cops manning one patrol car. In the case of the sandwich though, it was a two-layer beast of a sandwich.

"We'd get corned beef brisket and slow roast them. It makes the corned beef so tender, it pulled away like pulled pork. This was real corned beef, and the taste was just excellent," Ryno said. "We made everything good. We made a chicken salad and called it the Stool Pigeon Sandwich. It was normal chicken, a few pecans, cranberries. Our sandwiches were on our own bread. We had fun names on all our food."

The menu evolved over the years. By the time the café closed in the fall of 2018, the café was serving up excellent perch for a Friday night fish fry.

But it was around that time that the bakery was consolidating all the baking production in Clare. The bakery needed more room for the loaves of bread, and Sherry—who had pointed out to Ryno many times that the café was a loss leader—became more forceful and said it was time to cut bait.

"It was a tough decision to shut it down but we had to have the space," Ryno said.

Fish, loaves . . . maybe if there'd been a little wine, it could have worked?

Chapter 9
FIFTY WAYS TO SELL A DOUGHNUT

From its very first day, Cops & Doughnuts hit the marketing jackpot—on social media, in newspapers, TV shows, commercials, magazines, on the Internet.

And why not? People can't resist a feel-good story—and the cops make it easy with their corny videos, media appearances, and silly stunts. Sometimes, they'd riff on the cop-to-the-rescue theme—speeding a missing bran muffin to a company party, for example. And then there were the skits with a Dean Martin/Jerry Lewis kind of flare. In a recent commercial, Bubba played the goofball chemist, blowing up his new doughnut formula, and Ryno, the straight man, sighing in exasperation.

Ryno, Mr. Winkler, and Bubba making a TV commercial at Clare High School.

The bakery set the tone at its first grand opening.

"This isn't just a bakery," Bubba announced. "It's a *cop-owned* bakery."

They created a press conference to look like a major crime scene, surrounded by "Do Not Cross" yellow police tape.

State Representative Tim Moore welcomes Cops & Doughnuts to the neighborhood.

"We put a podium right out on the sidewalk and we ran the press conference just the same as if we'd just busted a serial killer," Ryno said. "Bubba and I used to write a lot of news releases for press conferences, and that's exactly how we approached Cops & Doughnuts."

They've used police tape ever since, creating

Ryno proudly cuts the ribbon, aka police tape.

an area in front of the bakery to get attention—a kissing booth, an air guitar booth, a time-out booth, you name it.

Ryno and Bubba are often called marketing geniuses and rightfully so. Few people put more effort into promoting doughnuts and no one has more fun. The results speak for themselves. Each year, some 400,000 people come into the Clare bakery, and the number is expected to rise close to 500,000 in 2022.

COPS & DOUGHNUTS

The kissing booth: love at first fritter.

Sidewalk therapy

On some days, 5,000 people come through the bakery doors.

Ryno and Bubba embrace their goofiness, their nerdiness. Most of all, they're authentic, said Jim McBryde, CEO of the Middle Michigan Development Corporation.

And it's their authenticity that appeals to the hardest-to-get generations: millennials and Gen Z, who are looking for authenticity more than anything else, he said.

"If you put up a really good doughnut store and you've got a story and it's on the bus stop for senior citizens, you're going to get the boomers and the Gen Xers. But the key to it is, how do you get that next generation? How do you get the millennials? How do you get the Gen Zs? These guys figured it out. They are authentic. I don't know how they did it, but they figured it out.

"This younger crowd, millennials and Gen Z, they're on the Internet an incredible amount. They watch YouTube. They look at social media heavily. And when they sense authenticity in someone or something or some business endeavor, it clicks that these guys are for real. They're funny, they're engaging. 'This is not like a big sell. They're trying to make me laugh.'"

Neither Bubba nor Ryno were trained in marketing, but they recall an early love for pizazz. Bubba remembers getting a .22 rifle from his dad for his tenth birthday. He was impressed with the image on the ammunition box—a yellow jacket resting on a hollow-nosed caliber—and imagined going into advertising. Little did he know that he'd be in front of a camera with a hard hat on, acting like a goofball on a daily basis.

Ryno had dreams of becoming a reporter—the first to know what's going on, the first to announce news to the world. And now he's on Facebook and television, reporting bad weather, traffic accidents, and doughnut news.

Bubba and Ryno are constantly brainstorming ideas on how to get people's attention using cop humor. An early, brilliant idea in September of 2009 was drawing an outline around Bubba in front of the bakery, with the words "9-5-2009, Bubba down."

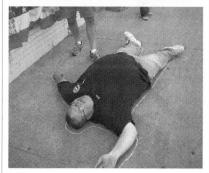

Sidewalk cop humor, admittedly dark.

Ryno spends at *least* four hours a day on Facebook and Twitter, seven days a week, while Bubba handles outreach to all kinds of groups. When it comes to videos for Facebook or TV commercials, they perform like a well-greased team.

"Usually, Ryno's the straight guy and I'm the idiot," Bubba explained. "He's always saying, 'Bubba, *what* are you doing?' And those *usually* go over better than when I'm the straight guy."

"You know you've heard of good cop, bad cop?" Ryno asked. "We play the smart cop, dumb cop. That's just the way we do it."

Ryno has found his gift with social media and Internet marketing. He's even taught marketing classes.

"Here's a man with, well, I don't want to say little education, I mean, he's educated, but Ryno is a wizard," said Clare Mayor Pat Humphrey. "As far as marketing goes, I've never seen anyone like him. He'll be sitting there and say let's do a video. They'll do some crazy thing, and it's all ad-libbed. People love it."

The cops spend exponentially more money on marketing than the original owner, whose yearly ad budget totaled $79.50. A single Cops & Doughnuts billboard cost ten times that for one month and the cop owners lease ten year-round billboards every year.

That said, the cops are frugal and make every penny count with creativity, humor, and imagination. Here's how they lure thousands of people to exit off the freeway and drive to downtown Clare for a tasty doughnut.

SOCIAL MEDIA

The biggest advertising value by far, Ryno said, are Facebook ads. Every post has the potential to reach thousands of peo-

A family braves a snowstorm in fashionable beachwear, a small sacrifice for warm doughnuts on a winter's day.

ple for a few dollars. The ads allow him to define exactly who will see the ad, their age, gender, and whether they like to eat doughnuts. Well, maybe not that last one.

The two ex-cops spend a lot of time brainstorming goofy ideas for their Facebook page and leave nothing off the table. One winter day in 2014, during a two-week stretch of frigid temperatures, they did a Facebook promotion that invited everybody to wear their bikinis and beachwear into the bakery for a free doughnut. Unbelievably, a few people took them up on it, including a family that ended up on the Cops & Doughnuts Facebook page. Ryno and Bubba wore T-shirts, shorts and Hawaiian leis.

Bubba said when it comes to commercials and Facebook videos, they're shameless.

How shameless?

"I lost a bet one time about the business and ended up in

a pink tutu ballerina outfit and had to appear at an art gallery opening wearing it," Bubba said, still in a state of disbelief. "But it raised seven hundred dollars for girls' softball."

The pink tutu, surprisingly, doesn't even come close to a Facebook video promoting the bakery's new offering of Cornish pasties.

As Bubba and Ryno were brainstorming video ideas, they talked about how people mispronounce "pasties" all the time. There are the pasties (soft a) that you eat and pasties (long a) that strippers paste on their nipples.

"So, right off the bat, I came up with a really crazy idea," Bubba said

Five minutes later, he was standing shirtless before the bakery manager, whose unscheduled job that day was to tape shiny blue pasties onto Bubba's nipples. With his shirt off, the pasties ribbons swinging and the camera running, Bubba walked into the bakery from the back, announcing, "Hey, Ryno! I'm here for pastie day!"

"No Bubba, not pasties, it's pasties," Ryno said, pointing to a golden-brown pastie.

"Whoops!" Bubba said, his hands flying up to cover his pasties.

Ryno shook his head and invited viewers to come and try out their new pasties (with a soft a). The video has received no less than 142,000 views and hundreds of comments.

And take the frequent fender benders in front of the bakery. When Ryno and Bubba hear the telltale crunch of steel or see folks exchanging phone numbers outside the plate glass window, they put on safety helmets and orange reflective vests and walk outside to offer a hand.

"When the newspaper shows up, we're always bent over the car. Our butts must have been photographed hundreds of times at accident scenes. And no matter what angle the photographer takes the picture, our logos on our safety vests get in the photo," Bubba said.

They wear the same getup when they venture out in front of the bakery to do weather or traffic reports for a Facebook video.

"There was one time that there was talk of a big winter storm coming, so I went out in front and Bubba is taking a video of me. I started shoveling the bare sidewalk real fast and he goes, 'Ryno, what are you doing?' And I say, 'You know how they pretreat the roads with salt? Well, I'm getting ahead of the storm.' You know, it's so stupid, but we watch the numbers and they get more attention than the serious stuff."

And speaking of shame, they shamelessly post photos from friends on Facebook. Joshua Lator, the Mt. Pleasant State Police post commander, once sent Bubba a couple of pictures from a deer-hunting trip with his son, Michael. In one picture, Michael is sitting in a treestand eating a Cops & Doughnuts fritter. The other photo shows Michael with a deer he'd shot, holding his rifle and holding up a fritter.

Bubba put the photos on Facebook with a caption: "A scientific experiment has been done, and you stand a 100 percent better chance of harvesting a white-tail deer in northern Michigan if you eat a Cops & Doughnuts fritter than if you don't."

"It's just a lot of little stuff like that, that's really funny," Josh said. "It's just every day with friends enjoying the laughter of it, you know?"

GOOD DEEDS

Ryno and Bubba do good deeds because it feels good! After all, they're former cops and that's what most cops do. But, hey, if they get media attention, it's just frosting on the doughnut.

If someone calls the bakery with a doughnut complaint, they don't get defensive but seize the opportunity.

"I remember the one year that the Kopy Korner in Mount Pleasant called up and said, 'Hey, we just want to let you know that your apple paczki (paczki is plural) don't have any filling in them.'"

At the time, the large apple chunks were plugging up the filler tube, and a new employee—unfamiliar with their weight—hadn't caught on.

"So, I said, 'That's not right! We'll drive some down for you right now,'" Ryno said.

Ryno and Bubba jumped into a Cops & Doughnuts van (covered with a life-size photo of the nine cop owners) and rushed to the scene. They walked triumphantly into Kopy Korner with a white box full of a dozen paczki and introduced themselves as the president and vice president of Cops & Doughnuts.

"We want to make sure you're 100 percent satisfied!" Ryno announced.

Then there was a corporate party. An employee had driven thirty-five miles into Clare to pick up the order—a unique doughnut for each person—but it wasn't until the party started that she noticed a missing bran muffin. It happened to be what the big boss had ordered. A frantic call went into Cops & Doughnuts, and Ryno handled it.

"I said, 'No problem, we're on our way. We want you happy.'"

With no time to lose, Bubba sped 95 miles an hour to arrive before the party ended, while Ryno filmed and narrated the unfolding drama.

"We hustled in there and we took them their bran muffin, plus another dozen donuts for the unexpected. It really worked out well because then they put it in their newsletter that went out company-wide," Ryno said.

The two say "yes" to just about any request that comes along. Bubba remembered a call from the local health department.

"Hey, Bubba," she said. "We're holding the Big Latch-On and could use your help."

"A latch-on? What's that?" he asked.

"Well, on a certain day and time of the year, women from all over the world simultaneously breastfeed their babies to raise awareness of the health benefits of breast milk. There'll be hundreds of thousands of women doing this, and we're getting a group together. We wondered if you could provide doughnut holes for the women?"

"Now most businesses would look at that and say, 'Oh, OK, we can give you some doughnut holes.' But that's not how I think," Bubba said.

He asked where the women were going to gather.

"Oh, we haven't found a place yet," said the health department woman.

"Well, you just did," Bubba said.

A few weeks later, thirty-seven lactating women arrived at the bakery with their babies. Reporters from three television stations, a radio station, and the daily newspaper arrived to cover the event.

"They got huge press, and every article mentioned how they had all gathered at the Cops & Doughnuts bakery," Bubba said.

Bubba was equally welcoming to the National Honor Society of Clare Public Schools in February of 2020. They wanted to host a hands-on class for folks of all ages who needed a little extra help with their smartphone. They marketed it as, "Old Dogs—New Tricks!"

"It was really popular," Bubba said.

Bubba recalls being asked for a donation for a diaper drive. He did one better and not only donated diapers, but sent out a press release that anyone who brought a pack of diapers to the bakery would get a dozen free doughnuts. "We collected *thousands* of diapers," he said.

And then there was the time he bought cases of SlimFast just after New Year's Eve.

"That's the time everyone's resolutions kick in, so I went to Walmart and bought every case they had, and then we marked it down," Bubba said. "We did a press release. 'Come to Cops & Doughnuts. We've got the cheapest SlimFast anywhere. Start your New Year off right.' Which is funny coming from a doughnut shop. The press just eats up this stuff, right?"

WEBSITE

The nine cop owners decided right off that Cops & Doughnuts would reach far beyond Clare, and the easiest way to reach people was online.

Ryno recruited his son Lance, who'd taken a web design class, to build the first website. And it didn't take long before Ryno learned the beauty of a domain name. Sure, they'd call their website www.copsdoughnuts.com, but Ryno began creating different domain names that would quickly zip people to their website. His favorite story was inspired by a now-closed bakery.

"There was a place that opened in Louisville, Kentucky, called Police Doughnuts, and they made the news locally down there. And the local news guy says, 'Well, you're talking about franchising and going really big nationwide. Isn't there a place up in Michigan called Cops & Doughnuts? They've been going strong.' And the guy from Police Doughnuts says, 'Aw, it's small compared to us, and they're nothing for us to worry about.' Well, I seen that news clip because I have a monitor on Google. So, I got on the computer, and saw they were so sharp, they hadn't even bought their domain yet, policedoughnuts.com, so I went and bought it. By the time the news broadcast got over, it was ours. If somebody typed in policedoughnuts.com, it pushed them right to our website."

Ryno also learned to create spin-off websites to cut over to a popular doughnut. For example, google the word "fritter," and you're likely to hit on www.felonyfritter.com.

Ryno takes online sales to an entirely new level with paczki, a rich Polish doughnut with a hole in the middle for cream or fruit. People eat this half-pound delicacy in the month of February and March, which leads up to Fat Tuesday, a religious holiday that precedes Lent, when Catholics and non-Catholics alike give up a vice that bothers them, whether it's cigarettes, alcohol, or extremely rich doughnuts.

Years ago, Ryno and Bubba figured they could sell at least twice as many paczki online as they did in their brick-and-mortar bakeries, so they created a new domain: www.buypaczki.com. It pops up whenever someone does a google search for "paczki." Within seconds of clicking the link, they're delivered to the website: six paczki for $39.99, including shipping.

COPS & DOUGHNUTS

The sales results were jaw-dropping. In 2022, Cops & Doughnuts sold 46,000 paczki, including 22,000 that were shipped across the country. The website not only featured paczki, but also a video that showed how the bakery makes them.

"It's just really cool. We got the video idea from a lady who made them with a mixer just a couple of years ago and it got over seven million views. When you scroll down on our web page, you'll find our other products we ship—salt-rising bread, a brownie. And there's a live countdown to February 1 before people can start getting them."

The bakery also uses its email list to its advantage. On February 1, Ryno sent announcement emails to 15,000 people. "Hey folks, the paczki are ready to order!"

The bakery has a special website for its dark chocolate brownie: www.copsandcannabis.com for customers with the munchies.

"Or you can spell it the wrong way like the stoners do. And that takes you there, too," Ryno said.

Ryno employs a total of sixty-two domains at a cost of $620 a year.

"That might sound like a lot to somebody but it means we're steering people to our website in sixty-two different ways," he said.

Cops & Commercials (and Videos)

Ryno and Bubba love to make commercials and videos for their Facebook page—the goofier the better. Real cops, real doughnuts, real laughs.

Take the video they made for Motorcycle Awareness Month. Bubba arrives on a minibike and Ryno climbs on behind him, a recreation of the *Dumb and Dumber* minibike tour (if you haven't seen it, it's worth a google and a giggle).

Ryno's favorite version was when he and Bubba climbed onto a minibike and used a big fan, borrowed from a local bar, to blow back the tassels on the handlebars and sheets of toilet paper (wrapped around their necks) to make it look like they were moving. In fact, they were sitting on the minibike in the bakery alley and using a green screen. But to the viewer, they appeared to be pulling out of the parking lot of Jay's Sporting Goods.

Bubba and Ryno said the video got a lot of laughs but also complaints.

"We had people think that we were really driving a minibike," Ryno said. "I had a guy come in here and he says, 'What do you guys think you're doing, putting commercials out like that, teaching people they can drive the wrong way?' I said, 'It's not a street. It's a parking lot. And we weren't even there. We filmed it in the alley.'"

Another woman demanded they take the commercial off the air.

"What's wrong with it?" Bubba asked.

"Well, two guys your size should not be riding around on a little minibike like that. You don't even have real helmets on. You're wearing hard hats."

"Ma'am, it's all fake," said Bubba. "It's all to have fun. There's no way that little bike could hold the two of us on it."

"Well, little kids might think it's real," she insisted.

Bubba stood firm. He stood for humor.

"I appreciate your input, but we're not going to take the commercial down," Bubba said. "This kind of thing has happened

Bubba revs up his minibike for a hilarious, albeit occasionally misunderstood commercial.

several times when people didn't realize it's a joke. Ryno and I will do a bit like he's here in Clare and I'm in Bay City and we throw a doughnut to each other, and we catch the doughnut. And every time we do that, at least one person will say, 'Oh, that's so fake.'"

"One guy even said, 'That's so fake. You're throwing it to the north and Clare is to the *west* of Bay City,'" Ryno said.

For more real laughs, google "bloopers and Cops & Doughnuts ads" or visit copsdougnuts.com/video.

Media

It is a rare thing to get the kind of national media attention Cops & Doughnuts garnered in its first two weeks. An Associated Press story sent the bakery into the media stratosphere. To explain, the Associated Press is a wire service used by major newspapers, which cherry-pick from a daily pool of articles from across the country. One AP article can translate into views by millions of eyeballs just like the very first 2009 article about the bakery.

Media attention has never reached that level since then, but the cops find a way to stay in the news. Cops & Doughnuts is the go-to business for local reporters who have a deadline to meet.

"There are a lot of business people who don't want to be on camera. They turn down the reporters. They don't want the attention for multiple different reasons. Some of them are bashful," Ryno said. "Others don't want to have the health department see that they've got a health code violation they haven't fixed. It could be almost anything you can think of. There's just not a lot of people that want to have their face in the news."

"The reporters know we'll talk to them, and they come in even if the story has very little to do with Cops & Doughnuts," Bubba added. "They'll stop by and say, 'Hey, you want to talk about the hot weather this summer or the amount of traffic?' And they know we'll just walk up and talk to them. I think we're really good at it. I mean, I don't want to brag, but we know if they walk right over here, we're pretty darn good."

"The news has even started following *us* to get the news," Ryno added, "and I can prove a point on that. There's a bakery in Minnesota that raised their prices, saying they couldn't absorb the higher costs. We shared that on Facebook a little over a week ago. It took off so well that TV 5 out of Saginaw seen it, and I did an interview with them last week about it. That's because they're following our page, and then they get a hold of us for the news. We've become one of their sources."

The cops often brainstorm what might get some attention. When the cops bought a third building on the block to expand the bakery space, they took down the sign for the now-closed Chinese restaurant and decided to create a little drama.

"We covered the window with plastic to mess with people," Ryno said. "Everybody was always guessing what we were going to do next, so we put a sign up: Coming Soon! Cops and?"

"It was all marketing, because we knew it was going to be the Traffic Stop Diner, but we just wanted to keep everyone guessing!" Ryno said.

The entire City of Clare began guessing what the crazy cop owners were going to come up with next. Lucky for the bakery, the volunteers from the Clare Fire Department decided to play a prank. Late one night, some jokesters snuck down and put a big sign over the "Cops and?" that read, "Coming soon, Cops and Strippers."

"Now that really got the town talking! It even made the front page of our local paper," said Ryno.

The cops made the AP wire when a microbrewery down the street created two specialty beers—Hoppy Cop and Coffee Cop. They infused a brown British ale with a fresh doughnut supplied by Cops & Doughnuts.

"We teamed up with them—Four Leaf Brewing—to do a doughnut beer," Bubba said. "They gave us what amounted to a tea bag, and we filled it with a sour cream doughnut and they steeped it in their brown British ale and came up with two brews—Hoppy Cop and Coffee Cop."

Four Leaf served up the beer by dipping the rim in a glaze and blue sprinkles. Voila!

Another AP article reported on the bakery's special delivery to a 108-year-old woman by the name of Bernice "Babcia" LaBoda. The story began when Babcia's granddaughter ordered a dozen doughnuts online and left a sweet note that she was buying them for her Polish grandma. The manager passed on her comment to Bubba and Ryno, who jumped in their van in February of 2021 to drive six and a half hours one way to La Moille, Illinois. They hand delivered the treat, along with a pink shirt that said, "Don't Glaze me bro" and a pink Cops & Doughnuts beanie.

Because of the pandemic, their visit was brief. Babcia was in one room and Bubba and Ryno in another. But they were able to smile and wave at each other. In the next two months, another thirty special birthday requests rolled in.

Dave Whittenbach, the co-winner of *Donut Showdown*, holds the winning tray of Driftwood doughnuts.

The cops have dozens of stories of TV appearances. There was the time when Cops & Doughnuts competed for a 30-second ad to appear on the Super Bowl. They were one of the last two finalists.

"I talked to the vice president of the company, and he said it came down to us and the other company. And it was a split decision. Wow. And the only reason they voted against us, is we took an existing business and made something out of it where the other business started from scratch."

Another time, two bakery employees competed on a food show

Tom Dalden, host of *Under the Radar Michigan*, mugs for the camera.

COPS & DOUGHNUTS

Behind bars: the TV crew of *Small Town Big Deal*.

Donut Showdown and split the prize of $10,000!

The cops were also featured in a TV show, *All Over the Place*, a British TV show aimed at 13-year-olds. The bakery made an appearance in the segment titled, "52 Quirky Travel Destinations in the USA." Closer to home, the bakery starred in *Under the Radar Michigan* and *Small Town Big Deal*.

The cops hit gold with a March 2013 article in *American Profile*, which was inserted in ten million newspapers across the country.

"That's the only time we'll be the centerfold probably," Bubba said, acknowledging that even his shiny blue pasties couldn't get him that kind of exposure.

"For years after that, we would have people come in. They had ripped out that story and saved it for when they took a trip to Michigan. And the other thing that's kind of a chuckle is when people come in and say, 'Hey, did you see this story in *American Profile*? And it's got our quotes in there.' Ah, yeah, we did see it," Ryno deadpanned.

Billboards

Remember the excitement of AP business reporter Matt Small, who thought Cops & Doughnuts would hit it big? He gave Bubba some invaluable advice.

"He told me, 'Your lives are going to change. You keep this going! This story is going to plant an image in everybody's mind that yes, they'll forget, but they'll be easily reminded. You put some billboards up so that as people travel along, and they'll think, 'Hey, there's that Cops & Doughnuts we heard about.'"

A Cops & Doughnuts billboard in Ocala, Florida.

Bubba recalls the thrill of seeing the first Cops & Doughnuts billboard with a photo of all nine cop owners.

"We hopped in Ryno's van to go to McDonald's, and we drove out in front of the sign.

A Cops & Doughnuts "Welcome to Michigan" billboard.

We put our four-way flasher on and ate our lunch, sitting illegally on the expressway. 'We're on a billboard; we've hit the big time now.'"

Celebrating their win on *Donut Showdown*.

COPS & DOUGHNUTS

And the billboards seem to work. Visitors to the bakery often talk about the billboard they spotted along the freeway.

"We're just willing to take a chance on them," Bubba said. "We have a billboard between Indianapolis and Chicago on I-65, and I had a whole family here, and they bought over $100 worth of stuff. They said they saw the billboard and asked, 'Why on earth do you have a billboard between Chicago and Indianapolis?' And I said, 'Well, you just answered the question. You're here, right?' It's just that billboards are very successful for us."

One of their most successful billboards can be seen off the freeway driving out of Frankenmuth, one of the biggest tourist locations in Michigan. They're planning to post another near Mackinaw City.

The bakery goes all out with backlit billboards on all three freeway approaches into Clare. The bakery is like a magnet for all the other businesses, who take advantage of the traffic they draw in.

"The owner of the Doherty Hotel used to lease a billboard but doesn't anymore," Ryno said. "He told me, 'What do we need them for when you're getting people off the exit? I'm the only hotel downtown, so where else are they going to stay?'" Ryno said.

The cops are always inventing new ways to get Cops & Doughnuts in front of eyeballs. Bubba hands out what looks like a driver's license with an image of a $100 bill paper-clipped to it to nearly everyone he meets.

"We give this out all the time; it's good for a free doughnut at any of our locations," Bubba said. "It's what we called the Chicago driver's license back in the day. It was commonplace

A reproduction of a Chicago bribe, good for one doughnut. A $100 bill is pictured on the back.

for people to clip a $100 bill onto their driver's license and hand it to the officer. And then the officer would bring back the license without the $100 bill or a ticket and say, 'Have a good morning,'" Bubba said.

"We never did that," Ryno hastened to add.

"Yeah, we never did that," Bubba said. "I had one person from a big city try to do that, and I let him have it. I chewed him out. I said, 'Don't you ever try this again. This is God's country up here. We don't do this stuff.'"

Their latest marketing strategy? Trash marketing. When they're traveling outside of Clare, Ryno or Bubba will strategically place an empty Cops & Doughnuts coffee cup atop a heap of garbage, hoping it will catch someone's eye.

COPS & DOUGHNUTS

Will a trash can sighting inspire a person to visit the website to buy a doughnut? Ryno and Bubba don't know. But they don't sweat it. They just pile on the marketing and watch their sweet doughnuts disappear from the shelves.

Chapter 10

THE POLITICS OF POLITICS

We all want to believe our fellow countrymen have a sense of humor. But when it comes to politics, hmmm, not so much. Bubba and Ryno can attest to that.

It all started with the 2016 presidential campaign, when most people were wringing their hands and, gasp, arguing with each other. Bubba and Ryno, on the other hand, decided to have a little fun and run for president—together. You'd get both of them! They announced their candidacy in February 2016 on the lawn of Clare's City Hall and soon started making goofy videos.

The men formed the LARD party. Lest you think it was inspired by a "lard and doughnut" platform, you would be wrong. It was the party of love, standing for "Love All Republicans and Democrats!"

With Midwestern earnestness, Bubba and Ryno promised to work with each other and reach across the aisle. Bubba would work on Mondays, Wednesdays, and Fridays, Ryno on Tuesdays, Thursdays, and Saturdays. On Sundays, they'd rest but remain on call.

"We promised to build a HUGE wall between the USA and Canada. A beautiful wall! To keep Canadian doughnuts out, and Tim Hortons was going to pay for it!" Bubba said.

COPS & DOUGHNUTS

Ryno claimed he was Democrat, while Bubba took on the mantle of a Republican. In reality, both Ryno and Bubba say they are independent and seek out their news from a range of sources to get a more balanced view of the world.

"You've gotta be independent when you're in business," Ryno said. "I think there's good stuff on both sides, bad stuff on both sides. But the two-party system has got us in the mess we're in, and I don't know if we'll ever get straightened out."

But are they truly independent? Ha! You'll have to come to the bakery's roundtable to know for sure.

In July 2016, Ryno and Bubba attended an event at Clare's Doherty Hotel. They were taken by a speech given by Kriste Kibbe Etue, a colonel at the time who oversaw the Michigan State Police force.

"She explained that Republicans were holding their convention in July in Cleveland and officials were expecting a lot of protesters. Cleveland was asking other states to send in officers because the election was so contentious and they were expecting trouble. So, the Michigan State Police was planning to send down a whole bunch of troopers to help with ground control and security," Bubba said.

"And then I have the idea that, 'Hey, you got a bunch of cops down there. I'll bet the state troopers would appreciate a little something from home like doughnuts!'"

Before the sun rose at 5:00 a.m. on July 17, Ryno and "Pete," the newly hired CEO of Cops & Doughnuts, loaded up their van with doughnuts and drove five hours down to Cleveland. Their Cops & Doughnuts van was fully "wrapped" with a photo of the nine cops and bakery logos galore to serve as a roving advertisement.

They arrived at 10 a.m. at ground zero of security near the Quicken Loans Arena, where the convention was being held. The van came to a stop at a red light, where the street was closed off.

"This was where Cleveland was running a little, like, mobile headquarters for the convention. The Secret Service and everybody was working just across the street from that," Ryno said.

Ryno sighted a middle-aged man wearing blue police pants with a white shirt. He figured he was the shift commander. The officer motioned to another cop, and they waved Ryno to drive over. Ryno couldn't quite read their expression, so he pulled up and jumped out of the van, fearing the officers were angry that he'd driven into the center of a tight security zone.

"But they weren't. They were great, and the guy in the white shirt was actually the deputy chief, number two in charge of the Cleveland Police Department."

He asked Pete and Ryno what they were doing.

"We're bringing the cops doughnuts!" Ryno said. "But we need a place to park, somewhere where we might get some good visibility with the van."

"Sure," said the officer. "We'll put you right in the city center, which is two blocks away."

And instead of giving them directions, the deputy chief got into a golf cart and led them over.

"He's making hand motions to the cops and they're jumping to attention and stopping traffic for us."

Ryno and Pete parked the van in the heart of the city and began handing out doughnuts to cops who had traveled from across the country, California included.

COPS & DOUGHNUTS

Cops & Doughnuts finds a great parking spot at the Republican National Convention in Cleveland.

"It was such a great spot and good advertising, we stayed about four or five hours," Ryno said.

The expected hordes of violent protestors never showed up, but there were a dozen standing near the van.

"I was talking to them, and everything was quiet and cool. But as soon as the news cameras showed up, they pulled out the signs and started making a ruckus. And when the cameras left, they picked up their things and they left, too.

"I saw an unmarked SUV, the Cleveland SWAT team, pull in ahead of them, but there were no problems. I watched the TV news later that night and they portrayed the convention as a powder keg. . . . It looked like there were hundreds of protestors. There really weren't. It was quite an experience."

Ryno poses with a Republican supporter.

When Ryno returned to Clare, he promoted the convention photos and video heavily on all their social media accounts.

"Then people started saying, 'Well, if you went to a Republican convention, are you going to go to the Democrat convention, too?'"

The cop owners agreed, and Bubba called the office of U.S. Senator Debbie Stabenow, a local hero who grew up in Clare. Stabenow was familiar with Cops & Doughnuts. In fact, she announced her Senate campaign at the bakery in 2018.

"Well, Debbie Stabenow is a friend of mine," Bubba said. "My mother was her piano teacher. We grew up here. So, we got a hold of Stabenow's office, and she put everything together for us."

Ryno and Bubba on the scene at the National Democratic Convention in Philadelphia.

Just a week after the July 17 Republican Convention, Bubba and Ryno loaded up the Cops & Doughnuts van and headed out to Philadelphia with 1,776 doughnuts in the back. Well, maybe not exactly that many, but it sounded good. They drove all night and Bubba was treated to the sight of a rosy, summer sunrise. It nearly blinded him, but it was a revelation.

"I'm not an early riser, so I was, 'Wow, this happens every day,'" Bubba said. "We got there, and they'd laid out the red carpet for us. They had assigned an officer when we got there to be our liaison."

They parked and were escorted into the Clarion Hotel, which had been transformed into Cop Central.

"They turned a big ballroom into an information center full of

Ryno and Bubba, posing with security police in front of the Clarion Hotel.

computers and cameras, watching all kinds of stuff. And it was where the cops would come in after an eight-hour shift and get something to eat. So, you had officers down there round-the-clock. There weren't any Michigan police, but there were cops from all over the country. And so we went in there and met with those guys and dropped off just a crap-ton of doughnuts for them. It was just a cool thing to do."

Bubba said organizers expected hundreds of violent protestors at both conventions, but they were peaceful.

"Was there no protest or violence because there was a large police presence, or was there nothing planned in the first place?" Bubba asked. "It's really hard to determine. But fortunately, it did not turn into anything serious."

COPS & DOUGHNUTS

After dropping off the doughnuts at the hotel, Bubba and Ryno drove around the outskirts of Philadelphia and handed out hundreds of doughnuts. No one had heard of Cops & Doughnuts, but that very fact made Bubba celebrate.

"We're happy when someone hasn't heard of us because that means we've still got room to grow," Bubba said. "It's like the story of the two salesmen who went to Australia to sell shoes to the Aborigines. The first salesman, who represents a lot of companies, calls his boss and says, 'Bad news. Nobody here even wears shoes.' The other salesman calls his boss and says, 'GREAT news, boss, nobody wears shoes!' It's all in your perspective, right?"

With Trump and Hillary Clinton now facing off, Ryno and Bubba posted another video on Facebook. They acknowledged a sobering reality. The LARD party didn't have a chance. So, they made a vow: they would throw all their support to either Hillary or Donald, whoever visited Clare first.

They created an invitation video for Trump, showing both Ryno and Bubba standing in a patch of golden, feathery pampas grass, about ten feet tall.

A screenshot Facebook video with a fake Trump and security guard. After the election, no one was laughing.

Ryno explained this was "pompous" grass, similar in appearance to Donald's hair. He and Bubba started petting it!

"Come on, Donald," Ryno said. "Come into our town. We've even got pompous grass that matches your hair. Come on and see us."

Next up was a video inviting Hillary to visit.

"It doesn't matter if you're having a medical episode and tripping off the curb. We've got a hospital one block away with a great emergency room."

The Facebook posts went wild with likes. By election day, no less than 275,000 people had watched their videos on Facebook and www.lardparty.org.

But just one day after Trump won the election, people's sense of humor upped and died.

"I'd posted a picture—a loaf of bread that looked like it had a big comb-over—and captioned it, 'Even our bread is starting to look like Trump.' This was one day after the election. Instant attack! People vowed to never come into the bakery again," Bubba said.

The ad was taken down within minutes. Lesson learned.

"It was immediately toxic, no matter which side we tried to play, so we stopped it all, like right now," Ryno said.

When the governor's race came around in 2018, Bubba and Ryno revived the LARD party and decided to make another political run.

Their promise?

"We're going to build a HUGE floating bridge from Manistee to Wisconsin, and the Green Bay Packers are going to pay for it!"

They also promised no more potholes and no more mosquitoes.

The video didn't get much traction, so Ryno and Bubba

went back to nonpolitical humor—the kind everyone was ready to enjoy.

Despite what the rest of the country was doing—taking political sides—the cop owners remained open to both sides of the political aisle. The bakery welcomed Governor Gretchen Whitmer twenty-four days into her term. She was the first governor to visit downtown Clare since John Engler and bought doughnuts, sat at the roundtable, and listened to people.

Ryno expressed his wish to keep the state's Pure Michigan budget intact. Whitmer agreed, and while the Pure Michigan budget was slashed in October of 2019 when state finances were stretched, it was fortunately reinstated in January of 2022 when the state ended the year with an extra $20.8 billion to spend on programs, according to a Jan. 14, 2022, *Detroit Free Press* article.

In addition to inviting Governor Whitmer into Clare, Ryno has also taken advantage of his Republican relationships, attending Governor Snyder's State of the State address in 2017 (he was guest of state Rep. Jason Wentworth). He also attended Trump's State of the Union in 2018 as a guest of Congressman John Moolenaar. He struck up a conversation with a gentleman who told Ryno he was a Wisconsin dairy farmer, but Ryno noticed his concealed weapon and guessed he was a Secret Service guy. His biggest regret: Trump's security took his phone so he couldn't take any pictures or video.

In 2016 when Bubba and Ryno jokingly ran for president, they could never have imagined how deep the partisan divide would become—the issue of cops often entering the conversation. Their only wish is that people can treat others with dignity and enjoy the company of their neighbors without politics getting in the way. They're hopeful that the image of cops coming together to give back to their community serves as a bright example of what the future could look like.

In the bigger picture, they feel listening to a diverse range of news sources and talking to each other over a cup of coffee and fresh doughnuts would do us all some good. And where better to do that than Cops & Doughnuts?

Chapter 11

HITTING A SPEED BUMP

Bubba and Ryno will always remember the years 2016 and 2017 as the "Speed Bump"—a financial tsunami that almost sunk the bakery. But as Bubba once said, a hard lesson learned is worth its weight in dough.

The slide began when a reserve police officer—let's call him Pete—served up a tempting offer to the nine cops: pay him a salary of around $200,000 to take the helm of Cops & Doughnuts and he would make the nine cops rich by opening franchises across the state. The cops believed him. After all, he was speaking from a place of proven experience: Pete had worked with two national fast-food restaurant chains for years.

Officer Richard "Junior" Ward said that the salary raised the cop owners' eyebrows, but they knew private sector salaries are higher than cops' pay. They felt he would be worth it. Even though Ryno was a talented marketer, he and the other eight cops were no experts when it came to expanding a business.

The irony is that Pete approached the cops in 2015, a year when Cops & Doughnuts was enjoying record revenues of approximately $2 million in sales. With website sales and heavy summer traffic, the tiny bakery employed a record high fifty employees. The cops even opened a Cops & Doughnuts bakery in Gaylord that year.

But Junior said most of the cops weren't all that happy. That's because Ryno—the bakery president—was a serious financial conservative. He was determined to protect the bakery's cash position. Instead of paying out dividends from the substantial profits, he reinvested in repairs, new equipment, the new bakery in Gaylord, and expanding the Clare bakery's square footage with the purchase of another storefront building.

Beaver said that it always seemed the bakery was strapped for cash. The cops had recouped their investment of $1,500 and were given free cell phones for a few years, but everybody thought they'd be earning *much* higher dividends after six years.

"We were always replacing equipment because things kept breaking," Beaver said. "You gotta remember, this bakery has been here forever, and nothing was new."

Another problem: managing expectations after the bakery garnered enormous national press coverage in the very first weeks. "We got that big inundation of press and popularity. We went from nothing to 100 right off the bat," Beaver said.

Added Junior: "There was a lot of buzz in the air. People thought we were going to be wealthy millionaires."

Originally the cops just wanted to make a couple of bucks, help the downtown, and keep the bakery open," Beaver said.

"If we got back our $100-a-month investment [for fifteen months], great," Beaver said. "But when everything went crazy after that first couple of years, our expectations totally changed, and after a few years, we just plateaued and things weren't expanding. We weren't getting the financial input into the business where we could really start making some money as owners yet. And it's like, come on, we want to do

COPS & DOUGHNUTS

something. And then [Pete] comes around and we all knew him and we knew his background. He had a lot of restaurant experience."

Beaver said he was open to hiring him, in part, because his own efforts didn't seem to be paying off—he often helped repair equipment and filled in when an employee didn't show up at the last minute. He didn't get paid for his work, but he said it wasn't an issue of money. He just got burned out.

"It just seemed like the bakery wasn't getting anywhere. We just kept hitting our heads against walls."

Pete pitched the franchise formula: simplify and standardize food production so that it's doable by lower-skilled, lower-paid workers; save money on bakery ingredients by making higher-volume purchases; and spread administrative costs over a larger number of retail stores.

He told the cops that Ryno—who didn't have a background in business—could only take the bakery so far, and he could take it to the next level.

Pete first proposed the franchise plan to Brian "Dogman" Gregory and Police Chief Dwayne "Midge" Miedzianowski, who then presented it to the other seven cops. His proposal was to open five new bakeries every year . . . forever if the cops were game.

"He said after five years, we'd have twenty-five bakeries and then he'd start paying each of us $100,000," Ryno said. "Everybody went along and drank the Kool-Aid."

The nine cops never officially voted on hiring Pete, but they all agreed on the hire, although Ryno had reservations.

"You know, I liked the guy," said Ryno. "We just all assumed that he knew everything, right? Well, what ended up happening is that he knew his little slice of the franchise business, but he didn't know enough to help us."

Before Pete stepped in, the cops had already opened their first Cops & Doughnuts "precinct"—a separate store attached to Jay's Sporting Goods in Gaylord. That expansion in the fall of 2015 felt natural and easy—they already had a great relationship with Jay's Sporting Goods in Clare, so it was a no-brainer to create their first precinct in Gaylord.

The Gaylord profits were high and for a key reason: the doughnuts and pastries were made in Clare and trucked north to Gaylord. The cops' only out-of-pocket costs were a cash register, doughnut cases, tables and chairs, gasoline, and wages for the counter person and driver. Cha-ching!

"It was highly successful from day one," Ryno said.

Pete proposed buying bakeries within driving distance of Clare in central and northern Michigan. Bubba was assigned to scout out bakeries listed for sale. In 2016, the bakery opened three precincts in quick succession: Ludington (May), Bay City (June), and South Bend (August).

The bakery used a cop shop naming scheme: Clare became known as the "headquarters" and each new bakery was called a "precinct." Gas stations and convenience stores that carried the doughnuts were called substations.

"I want to tell you why we picked the bakeries we did," Bubba said. "We used the same philosophy as Clare. Here's this old bakery that's going out of business, and the cops come in to save it. They've owned the bakery forever and didn't want to do it anymore, so that was our idea: we're going to rescue these bakeries, you know? It worked in Clare and, therefore, it had to work everywhere else."

COPS & DOUGHNUTS

Enthusiasm was high. M-Live ran a May 11, 2016, story headlined, "Small-town cops who saved a doughnut shop are building an empire."

Reporter Andrew Dodson asked Bubba if Cops & Doughnuts might someday be synonymous with Tim Hortons or Dunkin' Doughnuts.

"That's the plan, but it'll be better," Bubba said. "My guess is you won't see one on every corner, but I'd like to be in a lot of downtowns, supporting a lot of communities."

But it just didn't work out that way. The main problem? All three bakeries were producing their own product, which meant added costs of equipment repairs, salaries, and ingredients. Problem #2: it was too hard to standardize the baking operation and quality was uneven.

It might be easy to standardize cooking a fast-food hamburger, Ryno said; not so, doughnuts, pastries, and bread.

"[Pete] came from a place where you open up box 3942, that's got a yellow tag and that goes with box 34 and 93, you know, with a blue tag. And that's not what we are," Ryno said. "We actually make things from scratch, from formulas. Pete said he could take any kid and show them how to do it. Well, we knew that not to be true. And I think some of the other guys did, too, but they wanted to give him the benefit of the doubt, right? And yeah, he proved me right. So, he wanted me to disappear. And I did for six weeks. The other cops said I was interfering and causing too much trouble."

Travis Harrison, the bakery's CPA, grew worried over time when revenues lagged far behind the higher expenses of the three new bakeries. He began calling the cop owners together every month to show them the financials.

Although the original plan was to stay in Michigan, Cops & Doughnuts decided to buy a bakery in South Bend, Indiana. They opened the Dainty Maid Precinct with Mayor Pete Buttigieg personally welcoming the cops. But then disaster struck.

"The thing was, we did not do a good enough recon of the area," Beaver said. "We quickly learned they hated us, hated us down there in downtown South Bend. They're extremely anti-police down there."

On top of that, Notre Dame is a rival football team of University of Michigan—a team so reviled that some Michigan fans won't even drive through South Bend—and the hard feelings go both ways.

"We were not only cops, but *Michigan* cops," Ryno said. "We had that going against us. And then the other thing was the cops loved us, really loved us, and the sergeants and lieutenants, they'd come in and hang out. The customers wouldn't come in because the cops were there."

Bubba said they didn't sit back—they tried everything. A couple of weeks after they opened, for example, Ryno, Dogman and Beaver drove down with a van filled with bags of doughnut holes, each bag stapled and stickered with the South Bend address of Cops & Doughnuts to pass out at a Notre Dame football game.

The precinct of the Dainty Maid Bake Shop in South Bend, Indiana.

COPS & DOUGHNUTS

Even a billboard couldn't save the South Bend bakery.

"So, we go down there, we go right up in the middle of the thousands of people who come into the stadium, and we're handing all those free doughnuts out," Ryno said. "The Michigan people loved it, but I think that the Notre Dame people took it as a slap in the face. 'You've moved into our town and you've got Michigan all over everything.'"

Yep. The big yellow van touted "Downtown Clare, Michigan" with a photo of nine Michigan cops.

Notre Dame football fans couldn't stomach a Michigan-made doughnut shop.

"It was terrible," Ryno said. "It just didn't work. We lost more than four hundred and some thousand dollars in a short time down there."

There was nothing they could do right. Doughnut orders from the Notre

Dame campus evaporated from the first day the bakery ovens were fired up.

"When we bought the bakery, the old owner was regularly delivering cakes to dorms or whatever, birthday and graduation cakes. But I think the whole time we were open from August of '16 until November '17, we had one cake order that went to the university," Ryno said.

At the same time as the South Bend debacle, sales bottomed out at the Ludington bakery, albeit after a fabulous summer. Ludington, nestled on the sweeping shoreline of Lake Michigan, is a huge draw for tourists but virtually shuts down after Labor Day.

"I've got to say, Ludington was really the nail in the coffin," Beaver said.

The bakery had worked for the previous owners, because they had to pay only themselves in the slow months of fall and winter, Ryno said.

"Well, now we come over—we've got a mortgage because we bought 'em out and we've got labor," Ryno said. "The one good thing about it, even though we lost our butts, was we were able to let Mr. and Mrs. McDonald [the owners] retire comfortably because we paid them, and they had a good retirement. They'd been trying to sell it for nine years. So even though we lost our ass, we provided them a good retirement, you know, and I'm proud of it. It's sad that it didn't work."

And there's more . . . for years, public schools could only open their doors after Labor Day. But the state of Michigan changed the law right around the Speed Bump to allow them to open in August. This meant that families used to being able to travel and vacation until Labor Day ended their travels two weeks earlier, shortening what the cops called their "gravy season."

"Right as soon as that changed, we started slowing down in the middle of August. So now, you're only getting seventy-five good days over in Ludington," Ryno said.

And then there was the self-inflicted damage—the loss of two key personnel and the leadership they took with them. At the beginning, the eight cops asked Ryno to step aside as president. They wanted to give Pete the freedom to execute his plan without Ryno breathing down his neck. Ryno obliged and stayed home for six weeks. And when he came back, he was asked not to interfere.

The bakery also lost Sherry Kleinhardt, who was large and in charge at the bakery. She oversaw the entire operation, including hiring, baking, merchandise sales . . . everything. Her husband, Alan, worked for her, in maintenance, and they worked well together. She knew Pete wanted to expand, but things were heating up in the kitchen.

"When they hired Pete, I was told I won't have to do any more. I mean, I see the bigger picture. I knew they were going to expand. And it wasn't working that way. They were taking some of my staff for training in the other locations and, I don't know, I just couldn't do any more than I was doing. So I thought, you know, we'll let them do what they need to do or want to do. And well, I'm going to retire and enjoy life a little bit."

Travis Harrison

Travis Harrison, the bakery's CPA, sounded the earliest alarm that the cops were draining their cash reserves. Pete had lowered the employees' hourly wages, as promised, but the cost of labor and mortgages were climbing too fast.

Travis began advising Pete and the cops to go back to their wheelhouse. "Your pot of gold is right here in Clare," he told them. "Make the product in Clare and truck it out rather than spend loads of cash on bakery employees and equipment in several different locations."

He warned that South Bend was completely outside of the cops' "reputational zone." In other words, while most folks in Michigan had heard about Cops & Doughnuts, its fame hadn't necessarily spread beyond the state's borders.

"No one knew who they were. When [Pete] jumped into South Bend, that was way too far out."

Within weeks, the bakery in South Bend was bleeding cash. Pete's enormous salary didn't help.

"South Bend was a black hole," Travis said. "They couldn't get enough sales. The long story short, I told the cops you have to shut down South Bend. Cut the cord, like *now*. Otherwise, you'll go insolvent. There were times during all this that I had to spend extra time, daily, to manage cash flow, because they had so much cost into this expansion, so quickly. It almost crippled them."

Dogman had asked Pete a couple of times to shut South Bend down, but he refused.

Finally, the cops collectively came together before Thanksgiving to make a plan.

"During these hard times, we'd begun having meetings every week to get the guys aware, make decisions," Travis said. "I spent so much time to help them out, we were in this dire need. We finally, at one point, made the decision to let [Pete] go. His salary alone was ridiculous—two hundred thousand and some grand."

At that crucial November meeting, tempers flared, men yelled. Nine cops, nine alpha egos, nine investors—they felt let down and angry.

"There were some tough decisions that had to be made, and we made them, and then we fixed it," Gregory said.

Officer David "Grasshopper" Saad kept the peace at the meeting. Dogman agreed to order Pete to close South Bend and fire him on the eve of Thanksgiving.

Dogman's meeting with Pete was short and sweet—he knew what was coming down.

Even with all that, there was still a lot of digging out to do. In addition to closing South Bend, the cop owners also decided to shut down the Ludington bakery, where profits had gone south with the tourists. The fact was the tourist season was less than 100 days a year.

With Pete gone, Beaver and Dogman (both were working as full-time cops) and Bubba led the bakery operations.

They opened a new licensed bakery in Lansing in May 2018, which drew a first-day crowd of 4,500. (Despite this early-on success, the bakery burned out by the spring of 2020 for a whole slew of reasons.)

By September of 2018, the cops—at the advice of Travis—came together with a clear plan: run the business as a wheel. Clare would be the hub of production, driving out product in a concentric spoke to substations and precincts.

It was also around this time that Ryno became president of the bakery again, with Bubba as vice president. Sherry Kleinhardt rejoined the staff and quickly whipped operations back into shape.

The cop owners closed production in Bay City in September. They also agreed to immediately close their diner, the Traffic Stop—a lot of fun, but a loss leader, and they had to make room for the bakery's amped-up food production.

Yet cash flow remained an urgent problem. Travis told the cops they would have to hold a capital call in order to make payroll.

Beaver and Ryno injected cash immediately and looked everywhere for commercial loans. Ryno gave the cops until January 2019 to voluntarily invest whatever they could to save the business. The ownership then shifted percentage-wise according to the contribution amount.

The capital call was a hardship emotionally and financially: those who put in the most money—Beaver, Dogman, Ryno and Bubba—had to take out a second mortgage on their homes. The sacrifice hit Beaver particularly hard, as his deaf daughter required expensive financial support. They all mortgaged their homes to the hilt.

Meanwhile, Ryno scrambled to find loans for the faltering bakery.

"We borrowed money here, we borrowed money there. We had to, to make it work," Ryno said.

One person who really helped during this time was Tim McGregor, owner of C&O Sportswear in Mt. Pleasant, Michigan. C&O was the exclusive supplier for all of the cop shirts and other clothing. Even though Tim was owed a lot of money, he kept supplying merchandise so the cops could sell it. In the winter of their first year of operation, he did the same. Somehow, he could see the potential in these nine crazy cops and that the cops were doing their best to make it work. He never wavered with his support.

COPS & DOUGHNUTS

In the end, Travis said, the result was a fairer shake; the cops who had been putting in the most effort were awarded a greater ownership share to reflect their higher investment the second time around.

Cops & Doughnuts vans ready to deliver the goods.

Cops & Doughnuts not only survived but is now thriving. Every morning, two to three Cops & Doughnuts vans fan out to deliver bakery goods to the precincts of Bay City, Mount Pleasant, and Gaylord, and seven substations from Alpena in the north to St. Johns near Lansing.

The bakery is earning record profits and paying out the long-sought dividends. And their CPA is a happy man once again.

"They climbed right back to where they were, in fact, to a better position. And they brought back Sherry. She was the key to all this, running the production. She is phenomenal."

Chapter 12
FROM COOL IDEAS TO CLUNKERS

The bakery was a quiet place after the pandemic hit in the spring of 2020 and most Michigan businesses were shut down to limit the spread of the virus. The bakery was empty except for Bubba and Ryno, sitting alone at the bakery's roundtable and gazing through a pane window of sleet and slop. Brainstorming over cups of Morning Shift, they felt the warm light of an idea beaming in.

"You know, with all the people staying inside, people will be forced to talk to each other," Bubba said. "And maybe, ah, do other things."

Ryno laughed knowingly.

"I bet there's going to be a bumper crop of babies nine months from now."

"Hey, that gives me an idea," said Bubba. "How about we make a little infant onesie that reads, 'My parents didn't social distance.'"

"That's a *great* idea!" Ryno said.

Bubba calculated the product launch date—nine months from March 2020 with a few months added on for

A pandemic idea is born: a onesie!

good measure. At first blush, the market would seem too small (no pun intended), not to mention unpredictable. After all, no one knew then how long the pandemic would last. But come June 2021, the pandemic was still on everyone's mind. The staff loaded the onesies onto shelves and people bought them like hotcakes.

"People eat up anything that's funny," Bubba said. "We put them out in the windows, where people could see them, and all these brand new, first-time grandmothers, they couldn't buy enough of them. They thought that it was the cutest thing."

Another pandemic-inspired idea sold even better: a black T-shirt with an image of the Upper Peninsula. The tagline read: "Social distancing since 1837." The bakery sold a whopping 5,000.

The beauty of the Cops & Doughnuts operation is their speed of decision-making. No hoops to jump through. Just Bubba and Ryno or another cop owner coming up with an idea lightning quick—maybe bouncing it off Sherry, the bakery manager, or Dogman (the pragmatic ones of the bunch)—and executing it nearly as fast.

A pandemic-inspired T-shirt, celebrating Yoopers' attitude on social distancing.

"If we decide we want to do it, we do it. Like right now," Ryno said. "If you give us an idea for a new shirt that just tickles my fancy, I have such a good relationship with the screen printer, I can call him with an order, and he can have the shirts ready by tomorrow afternoon. When some other business is still looking at the idea, working out the numbers, getting a vote, we've already got it in the store."

Bubba and Ryno usually know within a week if they have a winner or a wash-out. If it flops, they tread down to the basement and pull out their "clearance" signs. If it's a winner, they double down on their investment by not only ordering more for the store, but also putting the merch on the website. Ryno will even create a new domain name like he did for the onesie: MyParentsDidntSocialDistance.com.

The onesies sold really well for three months, but sales plummeted along with the decline in COVID cases. "We hit it at just the right time," Bubba said.

The early days of selling merchandise were easy. Cops & Doughnuts stories were plastered all over national media, and clothing almost jumped off the shelves. People even offered to pay the cop owners for their business cards.

But later—during the financially challenging years of 2016 through 2019—they didn't have the luxury to gamble on far-fetched ideas.

"We only bought what we knew *for sure* was going to sell," Ryno said.

Throughout the ups and downs, Ryno and Bubba learned to listen to the cash register—what people were actually buying.

"You might think something is going to be a great seller, but remember it's not *you* who dictates the sale," Ryno said. "You need to adapt and bend to what the public wants."

Their best-selling products have been the colorful doughnut pillows, which people take home as souvenirs. Their No. 1 T-shirt says: "DWI: Doughnuts Were Involved."

COPS & DOUGHNUTS

"I think the reason is, people just like that bad boy persona," Ryno said.

Indeed. If you look around the bakery or on the website, a lot of their shirts and coffee cups carry "bad boy" slogans like "We Frisk our Fritters." Or the onesie that says, "Just did nine months on the inside." Bubba and Ryno are ex-cops with an admitted fondness for off-color humor. Listen in, for example, to this brainstorming session.

"How about if we were to hire a couple of kids, and they could go around and pick up all the perfect dog turds around here and then put them in a food dehydrator. Then we could spray 'em with a polyurethane coating," Ryno said. "We could bag 'em up, and the women would just fall in love with it. We could sell 'em as official police canine feces. You're laughing, but I'm absolutely telling you it would be a bestseller."

"We could call it Swiper Nuggets," Bubba said, "after that one dog Swiper down at the department. One of the best dogs that Dogman ever had."

"But I wouldn't put an exact name on it," Ryno said. "You know, just call it 'Official canine feces from a police dog near you.'"

If you think this idea seems far-fetched, Bubba said there's a moose-dropping festival in Alaska. "People collect moose turds and bake them hard and varnish them. They make necklaces and bracelets, all kinds of stuff out of them."

This is Cops & Doughnuts product development in the works! Herewith are some of their winningest and most woeful decisions.

WINNINGEST IDEAS
The Squealer and His Cousin Vinnie

Bubba is proud of two delectables that aren't considered the bakery's bestsellers, but are the most talked about: the Squealer and His Cousin Vinnie. First came the squealer—a long john with maple frosting, topped with bacon strips. One morning, Bubba was working in the Bay City location and noticed the Squealers had sold out. He asked a young baker if she could throw together a few more (this was during the time when the Bay City bakery was still frying and baking up its own doughnuts and bread).

"I can't," she said. "I'm out of long johns."

"Can we put them on Bismarcks?"

"We're out of Bismarcks, too."

"Well, what *do* we have?"

"Cinnamon rolls," she said.

"Okay, do it!"

"Sure," she said. "What do you want to call it?"

"I don't know. Let's call it Cousin Vinnie, Squealer's cousin from the old neighborhood. Bodda boom, bodda bing!"

Weirdly and soon afterward, a man called the bakery from Las Vegas and asked for a bunch of Squealers to get delivered overnight.

"No can do," Bubba said. "There's bacon on them, and we can't ship meat in the mail because of the twelve-hour shelf life."

After Bubba hung up, he thought about the flight he was about to take to Las Vegas in a few days with his wife. So, he loaded up a white bag of Squealers into his carry-on, boarded the plane to Vegas, and he and his wife drove up to the man's home. He knocked on his door and said, "Were you the one who wanted Squealers? Well, here they are!"

"He was shocked to see us. I think to this day, he thinks that we flew to Vegas just for him," Bubba said.

Cops Cash ATM

Cops & Doughnuts offers customers the convenience of an in-bakery ATM, which makes tourists happy. They prefer drawing out large sums of cash in a safe place and hearing Ryno's and Bubba's wisecracks: "It's guaranteed not to be counterfeit today."

CLUNKERS
40-Cal Jeans

As far as *total* failures, the 40-Cal Jeans landed at the top of the clothes heap. In 2009, the first year the bakery opened, they learned a clothing store was closing its doors.

"They had a whole crap-ton—that's a police term—of jeans left over," Bubba said. "And I had the brilliant idea that we'd buy all these jeans that he's got left cheap and go out to a shooting range and put 40-caliber holes in them. And then we'd embroider '40 Cal' on the back pocket because they were shot with 40-caliber handguns.

"We figured people would want to wear jeans with bullet holes in them."

So Bubba and Ryno took the jeans out to a shooting range and let the bullets fly. They quickly learned to aim away from the zipper. Once the shooting-fest was over, they loaded the jeans onto the bakery shelves only to realize that the left-over jeans were left over *precisely* because they didn't fit anyone. They were either enormous with a 72-inch waist or very small.

Out of the hundreds of pairs they'd bought, only four pair were of normal size. Those sold quickly, indicating that the 40-Cal jeans would have done okay if they had actually fit someone. The cop owners will never know. They

Dogman takes aims at the 40-Cal jeans, careful to avoid shooting out the zipper.

do know they lost $4,000 on this bad idea.

"We couldn't sell any!" Bubba said. "We lost our butts on it. It was a dismal failure. Nobody wanted them, but it was really fun shooting holes in 'em."

A Facebook Failure

Not all clunkers have to do with merchandise.

"I remember when we did a post on Facebook," said Rich "Junior" Ward. "It was Defense Attorney Appreciation Day, and we posted an offer, 'Buy one doughnut for the price of two.' And we got backlash saying, 'You legally can't do that!' But we're like, 'It's a joke. We're not actually doing it.' People get offended so easily, but I thought it was hilarious."

A Swimming Suit Hits Bottom

And then there was the swimming suit incident, which could

have been avoided had a few women been asked for their opinion. But, no, Ryno went it alone and chose a sleek racing swimsuit that he saw on a model in a magazine. Like all racing styles, it was skin tight—good for minimizing muscle vibration (and thus drag). It looked fantastic on the model, but didn't appeal to women who didn't want their body parts completely flattened.

"They were a flop, no pun intended," Ryno said.

Mopping Up Golf Towels

An odd choice on the face of it. Golf towels? Do cops love to play golf? No matter. The towels were a flop, too.

Ryno and Bubba put a Cops & Doughnuts logo on white golf towels—which (for all of you non-golfing readers) attach to a golf bag and are useful for drying sweaty hands or water-drenched balls. A golf outing was coming up, so they sent out two of their "cutest gals" to the golf course with bags of doughnut holes and towels.

This Cops & Doughnuts swimsuit looks fantastic on this model—but bakery customers didn't buy it.

"Well, we quickly found that in these golf outings, they don't care about breakfast food," Ryno said. "They drink beer, and they didn't want the doughnut holes in their bellies soaking up all of the beer. So I got called and they said, 'We've only sold a half dozen doughnut holes and no towels, and they're all out on the course golfing now.' We said, 'Well start giving away the doughnut holes and keep trying to sell the towels.'"

By the end of day, they returned dejected, reporting only two towels sold. Even those, they said, were bought out of pity. Bubba and Ryno nodded at the bad news. They descended into the basement to fetch the clearance signs.

Cops & Doughnuts Perfume

The cops decided to sell a line of perfume and did it right this time. They gathered a few women at the bakery together to test whiff fragrances for a new line of Cops & Doughnuts perfume.

They made their top picks and then brainstormed some names, coming up with "Probable Cause" for the women's fragrance, "Under Suspicion" for men, and for the younger women, "Miss Behavin'."

"I did like 'Incorrigible,'" Ryno said. "But we were afraid that a lot of the population wouldn't know what it meant."

The perfumes sold pretty well—it wasn't actually a fragrant failure—but the bakery quickly lost its Michigan supplier, forcing the cop owners to put a stopper on the whole idea.

Bugs and Doughnuts Don't Mix

The story of this failure starts with a massive June bug infestation on Clare's main street in 2013.

"June bugs were all over the sidewalk," Bubba said. "Every business person, almost every morning, was brushing these dead bugs off the sidewalks and into the gutter. So, one day, I'm just kind of chilling, sitting on the sidewalk, and I look over to the corner of our building and there's a whole pile of June bugs. I'm always thinking about marketing and decide to get a couple of long johns and decorate them with June bugs."

So Bubba placed the dead bugs—bearing a striking resemblance to pecans—in a straight line atop a long john with white frosting. Ryno took a photo and put it up on Facebook with a smart-aleck caption: "With all the June bugs this year, we decided to add some protein to our doughnuts today."

But no one was laughing. They were mortified, Bubba said.

"And then Ryno says, 'Well, hang on a second.' So he does some research, and he finds out the Chippewa Indians used to roast June bugs this time of year and eat them like popcorn. He puts a link to the article with a caption something like, 'See! These are edible!' The comments got even worse: 'I'll never come into your place!' or 'If I see a bug on a doughnut when I walk in, I am immediately leaving.'"

"That's an example of something that looked fun, but our customers didn't agree," Bubba said. "It was awful."

The Cream and White T-shirts didn't go over at a football game but eventually sold at the bakery.

Flunking Out at CMU

Here's a funny/not funny one. It was the year 2012 when the cop owners lost a solid wad of cash on fritters and shirts that they tried to sell at a Central Michigan University/Michigan State University game. They stationed themselves at the Wayside Central Bar near the college kids' hot spot and Kelly/ Shorts Stadium.

"So, we took the spirit shirts and called them 'cream and white' and 'macaroon and gold,'" Bubba said. "We took them all down there with Dogman and his wife, Denise, and we're all set up, and nothing sold except for one dozen to this one guy."

"So we start investigating," Ryno added, "and come to find out that the university is just down the road, giving away free T-shirts and then over the hill, all the banks from East Lansing had set up hospitality tents and were giving away free food."

"Yeah, people are walking right by us because they know there's free food on the other side, and the students are coming down because they're getting free T-shirts before they go in," Bubba said.

The cop owners ended up selling the shirts eventually, so no loss there. But a lot of wasted time.

The Cops Get a Tip

Bubba once put out a tip jar on the counter of the ill-fated South Bend, Indiana, bakery with a little sign: "Bail or Bribes."

Again people took it a little too seriously.

"I think they thought we're really giving away the tip money for bribes, right? Because, you know, it's a bigger city and that stuff goes on," Bubba said.

"And then there was our problem with our uniforms. We put the workers in orange inmate shirts that they thought was disgraceful, that we would make them wear them. Or maybe they thought we were hiring convicts or something. You know, the employees didn't have a problem with it, but the customers did."

And at Cops & Doughnuts, customers make the laws.

Chapter 13

CATCHING CRIMINALS

It defies all manner of common sense, but there have been several folks—bakery employees—who have lied, stolen and even used a Cops & Doughnuts van to make a drug stop.

The bakery has a fun-loving counter staff, but the cop owners are serious about bringing embezzlers to justice.

Perhaps these brazen individuals were fooled by the light-hearted atmosphere, the fun-loving feel of cop collectibles, hilarious T-shirts, and the jail-themed bathroom doors.

If so, they obviously missed the serious side to the bakery and the fact that the cop owners have notable experience with catching criminals. Security is tight, with surveillance cameras inside and out of the Clare bakery, as well as at the other three precincts and nine substations. (In fact, Ryno pulls up his security camera to peek in on the dozen or so retired Michigan State troopers who gather at the Cops & Doughnuts precinct in Mount Pleasant every Monday and Friday morning, just to see who's showing up.)

Besides cameras and experience, cops are naturally suspicious, always on guard for telltale signs of nefarious intent. Yet they can't count on their intuition as a firewall against hiring thieves and liars. Bubba admits that a job interview isn't always the best predictor of how someone will work out.

"I look at everybody like I'm a cop because I was a cop," Bubba said. "But I have to admit, some of the hires have really surprised me."

Security cameras on the bakery's exterior keep a vigilant eye on downtown streets and sidewalks.

Bubba is talking about general employee performance—beyond guessing whether someone will lie and steal. Some employees who were phenomenal in the interview weren't the rock stars he expected. And the other way around. Gleaning whether someone will steal is a whole other matter. It's not always easy to monitor the dozens of employees 24/7. Many of them—like the delivery drivers—are completely out of sight.

Take the first two years, when the cop owners were extremely busy handling the onslaught of customers, hiring employees, and replacing decades-old equipment.

Sherry—the bakery manager—and Ryno noticed that money seemed to be missing from the cash box, which was kept in an unlocked office cabinet at the time. It looked like an inside job—there was no indication of a break-in. There were only two ways in and out of the office, both locked: a front door through the bakery and a rarely used back door that opened up into the back hall.

Bubba decided to set a simple mousetrap. He put a tiny piece of paper on the top of the back door. If someone opened it, the paper would fall to the ground which is exactly where he found it the next day.

At that point, the bakery had no security cameras, so Ryno walked down the street and bought a motion-activated web-cam at Clare Electronics. He placed it atop the office computer and concealed it with a piece of cardboard, so the intruder wouldn't notice it. The same night, someone broke into the office, using a screwdriver to reach in between the door and the frame and pressure the lock to slide away. The intruder walked over to an unlocked cabinet and pulled out a stack of cash.

"So, we see this guy, he's got his hoodie pulled up over his head like he knew there were cameras in there, but that somehow we wouldn't recognize he was our doughnut maker," Bubba said.

Ryno and Bubba were disappointed. They knew he was a questionable hire—he'd already spent time in prison for larceny in a building. But they wanted to give him a second chance. They hired his cousin, too, also a convicted felon.

"When we hired them, we told them both, 'We know you don't want to make doughnuts the rest of your life. But give us a year, give it a chance. Work really hard, do great, and what better reference could you have than from nine cops?'" Bubba said.

Fortunately, the thief's cousin made a wiser decision. He worked hard and stayed with the bakery for two years.

"And we gave him a good recommendation," Bubba said. "The last I knew, he was working in a factory and earning good money with full benefits."

The culprit stole more than $800, and Bubba and Ryno worried that he likely had taken much more—they'll never know. But they decided to turn it into a positive and wrote a press release with a headline that read something like, "Bakery Cops Get Their Man." The *Morning Sun* wrote a story, which the Associated Press picked up. It ran across the country and online sales ticked upward.

"We got thousands of dollars of free publicity with all the articles that ran. So, when he finally paid back the eight hundred dollars that he stole, we donated it to Clare's fireworks fund," Ryno said. "We use safes now. But they can only stop some people from stealing. Employees who have access can still get into them."

In fact, in February of 2022, the cops fired a shift manager for embezzlement. The baffling thing, though, was she did a super job and got along with everyone.

"This woman was a great employee, she rocked, but she had a gambling problem, and we didn't know it," Ryno said. "She was taking $150 to $200 a day from us, and everything was coming up short, but she was so smooth the way she did it.

"She was so good at her job that management didn't want to admit it was really happening, but all signs pointed toward her. We knew it had been going on for a while, and we just kept trying to set the traps. We took money responsibilities away from her in certain areas. And where she still had responsibilities, those were the areas the money was coming up missing. So it was just a matter of a process of elimination."

Again, cameras came into play and captured the woman arriving at the office at the beginning of her night shift. She took cash out of the safe, neatly folded it, and slipped it into her pockets. As she left to go home, she slipped even more money into her pockets.

"We got new cameras, almost like you're looking through a spotting scope, it brightens everything up," Ryno said. "She would come in, open the safe, act like she was closing it, and turn the light off. She could feel where she put bills, and we saw her put it in the pocket of her hoodie."

Another technique: She would change out the tills, but not before pulling one bill out of each pack of tens and twenties.

She was also filmed taking money out of the till and replacing it with "Clare cash" from the safe so no one would be the wiser. The cop owners captured three different incidents of thievery before terminating her.

The Michigan State Police in Mount Pleasant is handling the investigation (as it has in all of these cases), as other cop owners still work with Clare Police Department and the Clare County Sheriff's Department. So far, the fired manager has denied everything, despite the fact the video caught her red-handed.

In another instance, a bakery employee was stealing money out of co-workers' purses, which were all kept in a secure area. When she would go back to fetch her own purse, she fished money out of her colleagues' wallets. Luckily, her thefts were all captured on video.

"The state police investigated, and she fessed up," Ryno said.

The woman's boyfriend drove for the bakery and got caught using $700 from his gas card, drawing it out from an ATM at a casino, where he used the money to gamble. Travis, the bakery's CPA, noticed the illegal ATM withdrawal the next day. He notified the cops and the casino, who ran surveillance video and immediately confirmed the robbery. When he was confronted, he was less than contrite.

"He said, 'Well, you gave me the gas card to use, so I thought it was OK.' Wow," said Bubba.

Before the state police could charge him, he broke into a gun shop and stole a slew of guns in Saginaw and was charged with a federal crime.

"So, they didn't do anything with our piddly local state charges," Ryno said. "Sometimes when you have smaller charges in another jurisdiction, they don't even bother to mess around because they're going to get tangled up so long on the more serious charges."

The cops wrote the robbery off as a loss.

Bubba and Ryno remember the tip jar thief at the Gaylord substation. The employees noticed it first. Tips weren't as high as they should have been, and they quietly started counting the money before the shift and at the end. Someone was clearly dipping into the jar, so they alerted the manager, who started watching the cameras.

Sure enough, a young woman was taking tips when no one was around. She was immediately let go.

Speaking of open jars of money, a jar to collect money for a local fireworks fund was also robbed, Ryno said. That was the end of putting out collection jars for good causes.

A new-and-improved tip jar keeps cash secure.

COPS & DOUGHNUTS

Not all the bad actors have been thieves. Some thought they were doing a *good* thing. Take the clerk who waited on Ryno's family, who was visiting from Texas. Their first stop was Cops & Doughnuts. They picked out hoodies, T-shirts and gifts. Ryno's sister-in-law thought it odd when the clerk rang up only a few items and ballparked the bill at eighty dollars.

"This isn't right. All this costs at least two hundred dollars," she thought. She reported the weird transaction to the manager, who pulled the clerk aside to question her.

"What's going on? Why didn't you ring up each item?" she asked.

"Well, I did ring up some of the stuff, but I was just so busy, I didn't have time do it all. I just took a good guess so I could get through the line faster."

"She didn't work for us much longer. That's some of the issues we've had early on because we were so busy," Ryno said. "Who knows how much money we lost because of her doing that?"

There was one front-counter person at the Clare bakery who liked to give people a break on the price.

"She had a psychological issue," Ryno said. "It made her feel really good about herself when she could give people something. If someone came up to the counter to buy a shirt, say, she would ask if they were a teacher. If they said no, she'd ask if they were married to a teacher. If they still said no, she'd ask if they *knew* a teacher. If they said yes, she'd say, 'Well, today's your lucky day! You get a 20 percent discount!'

"Any time she could give something away, she would. If someone would come in and say, 'I need a dozen doughnuts.

I'm taking them over for my mom's ninetieth birthday,' she'd say, 'It's on the house!' Once we found out, we had to let her go. We talked later to one of her former bosses, and he said, 'That's the same thing she did at my drugstore!'"

At the South Bend bakery, a young woman was given a hat and two T-shirts—the Cops & Doughnuts uniform at the time.

"But then we caught her bringing out a bunch of T-shirts to take home that she thought she could have for free," Ryno said.

And then there were the manipulative wrongdoers.

In February of 2013, Ryno remembers a man in his sixties who came into the bakery but didn't seem to want anything in particular. He bought something but kept hanging around, looking at this, looking at that. One of the clerks, whose family worked for the sheriff's department, told Ryno and Bubba to be on the alert—she felt he was acting suspiciously.

"He was standing around for about an hour and my brother Tim and I were watching him. We saw he was looking at Bubba's books for sale. Picking one up, reading it, putting it back. And at one point, he lifts his shirt up, tucks a book into the back of his pants, and heads for the door."

As background, the bakery sells a wide range of books, including two written by Bubba about his life as a cop in Alaska.

So, Tim and Ryno followed the man out of the bakery. Ryno put his hand on his shoulder, and the fight was on. He kicked at Tim and then punched him in the face. Six officers were nearby, doing some training, and subdued him. The fracas brought the bakery manager out to the sidewalk.

"What did he steal?" she asked.

"One of Bubba's books. This one here," he said, showing her the book, *Alaska Behind Blue Eyes*.

179

"Ah, no, he actually paid for the book when he first came in," the manager said.

The man started yelling that he'd been unjustly treated and threatened to sue the bakery. He asked the police to call his attorney. As it turns out, Ryno and Bubba later learned the man had done something similar at other stores.

"We were set up," Ryno said. "We found out he did this all the time. It was his MO to make it look like he was stealing. He'd create a scene, and then threaten to sue. The attorney felt bad about it."

The matter, Ryno said, was settled out of court.

Over time, the cops installed several video cameras beyond the bakery's confines to help their fellow business owners investigate crimes.

"I positioned them for police work to cover the whole block and both intersections," Ryno said.

Those surveillance cameras came in handy when a couple shoplifted $20,000 worth of items from a jewelry store.

Ryno, who was notified immediately, pulled up the video and watched a man and woman climb into a van and drive northbound. He called the description in to the police, who arrested the couple and recovered some of the jewelry. They were later charged with a felony.

In another instance, a man threw a rock through the window of a gas station, busted in, and stole a few items. In the gas station video, he had covered his head, but it was possible to see his shorts and shoes. Eight minutes before the station's alarm went off, a man wearing the same shorts and shoes walked by the bakery, rock in hand, with two buddies, his lookout men.

Ryno shared the video with police, who started knocking on apartment doors and soon found and arrested them.

In 2013, the downtown and surrounding area suffered a spate of twenty-two robberies. This was when the bakery was open twenty-four hours a day. Ryno started piecing videos together and homed in on a vehicle, a red GM pickup, which was always in the vicinity at the time of each robbery.

"We pieced it altogether from the scenes, gave the police a description, and in less than twelve hours, the county's sheriff's department had stopped them."

Ryno and Bubba also used camera footage to find out who really caused an accident on a wintry day. An after-the-fact witness blamed a teenage girl, who was ticketed.

"Her mother called me and said, 'My daughter said there's no way that it happened the way they said it did.'"

Ryno reviewed the surveillance tape and saw that the daughter's story rang true. She had driven legally through a green light and was hit by another driver who had run a red light—she was going too fast to stop on the slick road. People who see only the tail end of a crash don't make good witnesses and are largely influenced by what people tell them, he said.

One day, the cops learned that one of the bakery drivers was stuck in snow and had called a wrecker to tow him out. But he was located on a gravel road, miles away from the doughnut delivery route.

"When we got to the bottom of the whole situation, we figured out he was running his drug route using our Cops & Doughnuts truck! It blows my mind," Bubba said. "Here we have some crackhead meeting with a drug dealer, bringing him dope, and in the background, is our van sitting in the driveway with full-size pictures of nine cops in uniform."

Bubba and Ryno made one video that should serve as a cautionary tale. It begins with suspenseful music and a would-be robber, a stocky man with a nylon stocking pulled over his head, walking into the bakery and shouting, "This is a hold-up!" Everyone—the customers in line, the counter staff—turn around, pull out their guns and aim at the man . . . just then, he slips on a jelly-filled doughnut and falls flat on the floor. An elderly woman scolds, "The place is called Cops & Doughnuts" like he's a complete idiot.

On a younger and more hopeful note, a four-year-old was admiring the collection of donated Matchbox cars one afternoon and slipped one in his pocket. When he got home, his mom discovered the stolen merchandise and marched him back into the bakery. The little guy, teary-eyed, stood before Bubba, stolen car in hand. Bubba crouched down to the little guy's level.

"Tell this man what you did," she said.

"I put the car in my pocket," he said.

"Well, I hope you learned you don't take things," Bubba told him. "I'm proud of you for telling the truth. Just don't do it ever again. OK?"

"OK."

The little boy handed Bubba the car. Bubba thanked him and gave him a card, good for one doughnut.

Chapter 14

LAUNCHING COPS & DOUGHNUTS INTO THE EDGE OF THE STRATOSPHERE

Back in the summer of 2015, Bubba came across a video of some Norwegian teens launching a doughnut into the edge of space using a weather balloon.

"I was instantly ticked off because I didn't think of it, and I wanted to do something like that. But who's going to remember the *second* person to send a doughnut into space?" Bubba said half seriously. "So then I thought about launching a coffee cup with our Cops & Doughnuts logo on it."

Bubba looked into it and realized that he might need a permit to send a cup into the edge of the stratosphere, double the height that commercial jets tend to traverse. Just around the time he was mulling it over, Mike Powell, a Boy Scouts of America representative, came into the bakery and asked for a donation to support area troops.

"We're planning to do some kind of science project, and I was hoping Cops & Doughnuts could help us out," he said to Bubba.

"Well, it's interesting you came in today," Bubba told him. "I was just watching a video of what these kids in Norway did, shooting a doughnut into the stratosphere. Maybe we could do something similar with a Cops & Doughnuts coffee cup."

Bubba and Mike sat down at the roundtable, where Bubba showed him the video. Mike immediately agreed the project was worth exploring.

"I'll make you a deal," Bubba said. "We'll buy everything that you need, the GoPro cameras, whatever. And if you do it, we as a company will give you a $1,000 donation and you get to keep the equipment that we bought."

The Boy Scouts went to work and also involved area elementary children who were signed up with the Students Participating in Academics and Recreation for Knowledge and Success (SPARKS) program. A total of about a hundred kids were involved.

"They had meetings and they learned about atmospheric pressure and weather balloons and the different layers of the atmosphere and GPS and all this kind of stuff," Ryno said. "It was amazing."

The launch was set for October 15, a cool and drizzly day. Scores of kids gathered in a park as Mike and two other men from the BSA prepared to launch a 20-ounce Cops & Doughnuts coffee cup with a BSA logo pasted onto it.

The cup was glued onto the end of an 18-inch ruler, which was attached to a small Styrofoam cooler. A GoPro video camera peeked from a hole in the side of the cooler directly at the Cops & Doughnuts coffee cup and an altimeter. The other lens looked out of the cooler bottom to capture video of planet Earth. The men loaded up the cooler with an old cell phone with a GPS tracker, a toy astronaut, and hand warmers to keep the electronics warm enough to function.

The cooler after landing near Linwood.

"They did a real good job of researching and putting it together," Ryno said. "They studied all those different components about how cold it's going to be up there. You know, they didn't put in a thermometer, but that would have been kind of cool. I bet it got down to 65 below zero probably."

The men sealed up the cooler with clear tape and filled a large white weather balloon with helium.

"We need a countdown beginning at ten," Mike shouted to the kids, who were happy to oblige.

When they hit zero and yelled "blast off!" Mike let go of the weather balloon and the crowd cheered.

As the balloon reached the thin altitude at 84,000 feet, it swelled to forty feet wide and exploded. A parachute popped out and the Styrofoam basket fell to Earth.

"They were tracking it as it went up. But then it got so high, it got out of the signal range, which they knew was going to happen," Ryno said.

COPS & DOUGHNUTS

A photo of a Cops & Doughnuts coffee cup pictured against the curvature of Earth.

They thought it was going to land in Lapeer County, 116 miles to the southeast, but it landed about 45 miles due east.

"So they all were chasing after it. The Boy Scout leaders, well, they went south on I-75 thinking it was going to go that way. But it actually went basically straight east to Linwood, and then it came back down. They had other things to do that evening, so they told us exactly where it went down and asked us to get it."

Ryno and Bubba headed out straightaway and drove as close as they could to the latitude and longitude coordinates. They stopped at a soybean field, pulling into a driveway between two industrial buildings.

The farmer was out working in a pole barn that housed his tractors, getting his equipment ready for the harvest. He walked over to Ryno and Bubba, who were both wearing their Cops & Doughnuts shirts. Bubba started telling the whole story in his characteristically long-winded way, when the farmer interrupted.

"That thing is in my bean field, ain't it?"

"Yeah, it is," Ryno said.

"Well, go ahead and get it."

Bubba and Ryno retrieved it from a drainage ditch between the bean field and a wheat field and walked back to the farmer to show him how it all worked. He was appropriately impressed.

After the thirty-minute video was uploaded, the cops viewed with great pride the Cops & Doughnuts coffee cup against the curvature of Earth on breathtaking display.

"It was just beautiful," Bubba said.

To watch the video yourself, google "How the scouts reached the edge of space."

Chapter 15

LOCKED DOWN, BUT NOT LOCKED IN

COVID descended like a dark cloud in March of 2020. Like the rest of Michigan, Clare had turned into a ghost town, with deserted streets and sidewalks.

It was early on in the pandemic and health officials were still trying to get a grasp on the virus. They knew older, obese, and unhealthy folks died at higher rates, but weren't positive about how easily it would spread. All fifty governors grappled with how to respond.

McEwan Street emptied out in spring of 2020 and so did Cops & Doughnuts.

On March 23, with 1,000 cases on record and rising in Michigan, Governor Gretchen Whitmer issued a "stay home, stay safe" executive order. People were allowed to recreate outdoors and "essential" businesses remained open (grocery stores, pharmacies, and the like). But the order broadly banned in-person work that wasn't necessary to sustain or protect life.

Fortunately, Cops & Doughnuts qualified as essential; the bakery stayed open, quickly pivoting to baking mostly bread and setting up a take-out line.

"A few people asked, 'Why are you an essential business?' But we were one of the most essential businesses," Ryno said. "We were making bread and selling to the community. We had people drive in from Gladwin because there was no bread. Almost thirty miles away, driving just to get bread."

During the month of March, Bubba and Ryno saw customer numbers dwindle. They closed all their locations except Clare and stopped paying themselves. The bakery operated with a skeleton crew. Sherry Kleinhardt, the general manager, sent home all but herself and a dozen workers until business picked up again. She and the human resources manager worked the take-out counter from 5 a.m. until 1 p.m., at which time Bubba and Ryno took over, closing the bakery at 9. Matt Hamilton, the production supervisor, baked up to 124 loaves at a time to keep up with

Cops & Doughnuts was deemed an essential business.

demand, making mostly white, wheat, and rye. At times, there was a long line for bread.

Thanks to Travis, their always-at-the-ready CPA, Ryno learned of the Paycheck Protection Program—a $953 billion federal program that helped businesses and nonprofits cover payroll expenses through a series of loans. Those loans were forgiven if the workforce remained stable. Ryno immediately applied and qualified.

After eighteen days, the first PPP deposit hit the bank, and the bakery was able to bring back staff. Over the next couple of months, demand built up to hundreds of loaves each day.

"If the PPP money wouldn't have came when it did that first round, we would have gone bankrupt and closed, so thank God that it came through. And that was true nationwide for thousands of businesses," Ryno said.

Meanwhile, the cop owners worried how forced isolation would affect their diehard customers who were used to coming in every day for a warm, fresh doughnut and steaming cup of coffee.

"There were some people during this whole COVID thing who had nobody," said Beaver. "You know, you've got an eighty-five-year-old guy who doesn't have any kids, his wife died ten years ago, and he comes down to the bakery every day. And now it's taken away from him. What does he do? He just sits there at home and those thoughts fester in his brain."

Even in normal times, Bubba said, some of their customers barely make it through each day.

"When something like COVID hits, well, they don't necessarily kill themselves or cause harm to others. But they're struggling. Really struggling. People just have no idea. The bakery is a kind of refuge for them."

Bubba and Ryno brainstormed how they could continue to allow these few customers to come in, given the ban on indoor dining. They combed through the wording of the executive order and concluded that they could hold "job interviews."

"It was allowed, that's the honest to God truth, and that's what we told people. That they could come in, and interview with me for a job," Ryno said. "They all played along good and we never heard a thing about it."

Although not elderly or struggling, Carol and David Singer were two of the regulars who arrived at the bakery during those eerily quiet pandemic afternoons. The bakery's lights generally remained off and the shades drawn in the roundtable room, so as not to attract undue attention.

"Job interviews are a very long process sometimes, and we had to go in repeatedly. They were so gracious to let us purchase a doughnut and coffee, so we could have the interview," Carol said.

In truth, she and David, both in their 60s, had found ways to spend time with friends each day—like taking a walk. But the bakery gave them a relaxed, comfortable place to see old friends without the tension they felt in grocery stores.

"We saw two or three older gentlemen who truly had no one," Carol said. "Bubba and Ryno were life saving for them by allowing some sense of normalcy and human interaction."

Ryno, who doesn't like to be told what to do, chose not to wear a mask, but was careful to keep his distance from customers. Cops, he explained, usually aren't all that comfortable anyway when it comes to personal space.

In those early months, the bakery ensured people were distanced six feet apart and the counter staff was masked. Bakers in the back already worked so far apart, they didn't have to wear masks. Customers were required to enter in one door and leave out another. "They weren't cross mingling. We ran things by the book," Bubba said.

Meanwhile, he and Bubba tried to focus on the positive and do what they could to keep things fun. They took note, for example, of the strange human behavior they were observing. Take product shortages induced by irrational paranoia . . . to wit, toilet paper. People were binge buying them off store shelves, leaving some of the public empty-handed. Noticing the trend, Bubba went out and bought a "crap-ton" of really cheap toilet paper. He announced on Facebook that the bakery was giving away two rolls to the first people to come by, no doughnut (or bread) purchase necessary.

When the pandemic closed schools in March, Bubba and Ryno decided to teach kids the art of making a great doughnut. They made a live Facebook series video, "Learnin' with Bubba and Ryno."

In the nine episodes, they explained the science and math behind doughnut making: the growth and separation of yeast cells, how to measure ingredients, the difference between Celsius and Fahrenheit—it's all there. A whopping 16,000 out of 64,000 Facebook followers watched the first episode alone.

COOKIE KITS

In the early months of the pandemic, Sherry Kleinhardt, the bakery manager, worried about how grandparents were isolated from their grandkids for long periods of time. As a grandma and former daycare provider herself, she knew they wanted the little ones to know they were thinking of them. Easter was approaching, and she came up with a brilliant idea of connecting them in the sweetest way possible—cookie kits! Six plain sugar cookies cut into the shapes of eggs and easter bunnies, three colors of frosting, and sprinkles. She sold Bubba and Ryno on the idea, and the bakers were put to work!

"We didn't put it online because we didn't know how it was going to go, but the phone rang and rang," Ryno said. "Bubba and I were taking orders like you wouldn't believe. Grandparents were buying them for their grandkids and leaving them on the doorstep."

Within a ten-day period, the bakery sold 368 boxes of cookie kits, the vast majority getting shipped across the country. Thank you social media! It not only appealed to grandparents, but adults of all stripes.

"There was a woman who came in who didn't have any children or grandchildren, but there was a lot of young children in her neighborhood," Bubba said, "and I think I sold her nine boxes. She went around to all of her neighbors with little ones and just left them on the porch."

The idea was so popular that the cops followed

Bakery manager Sherry Kleinhardt came up with the idea of Easter cookie kits—a pandemic hit.

up with a Cops & Doughnuts cookie box with three badges, three round cookies, frosting and sprinkles.

"We sold some, but it didn't quite have the same appeal—maybe five a week," Ryno said.

Business slowly began climbing back. In the summer of 2021, three tour buses even made a stop—still a tiny fraction of the nearly one hundred buses that visited during peak years.

Despite their initial good cheer, the pandemic became grinding. In October 2020, the Sutherland Precinct in Bay City was charged with pandemic violations. And the bakery's struggles to buy supplies just seemed to get worse as time went on—peanut butter was especially hard to procure. Prices of supplies kept climbing, which drove doughnut prices higher.

The biggest challenge? Finding enough people to work. That's because—in part—the government, which paid out $24.5 billion in PPP support to Michigan businesses, also extended unemployment benefits to 2.4 million Michiganders—a total of $38 billion. But the money had an unintended consequence for businesses; thousands of workers decided not to return to work. For many, the pandemic benefits exceeded what they could earn working forty hours a week.

To lure workers back in, Cops & Doughnuts increased its wages, as did thousands of other businesses. (Those increases in wages and supplies ultimately forced the bakery—like so many other businesses—to increase prices in 2022, which created another problem: significant inflation.)

Even after the pandemic benefits ended on September 4, 2021, workers were *still* extremely difficult to find.

Sherry explained that the bakery historically has found it a challenge to find enough employees, although it's never been this tough. That's because full-time employees are needed in summer when business explodes. But those 40-hour-a-week jobs disappear or shrink to part-time employment during the cold months of winter, when tourist numbers drop. Very few workers can adapt their schedules or budgets from full-time to part-time.

Pandemic politics also began getting under people's skin. There were political fireworks over the governor's early mandates that banned public gatherings and required masks and social distancing, even outdoors.

Ken Hibl, the city manager of Clare, said there was no way the city could hold the annual Irish Festival parade, which historically draws more than 10,000 people each year to celebrate St. Patrick's Day.

"I'll always be remembered as the first guy to cancel the Irish Festival," Ken said, laughing.

The city wasn't allowed to use taxpayer money to support public events, such as the St. Patrick's Day event, due to state mandates.

"But we attempted as best we could within the state's COVID mandates to support our local business community," Ken said.

Months later, the city faced similar issues for the Summerfest in July. Ken announced that for specific city-run activities, it would require compliance with state directives, including social distancing, masking, and limiting the close gathering of crowds to no more than one hundred. Clare Mayor Pat Humphrey was in agreement.

"The governor put down rules. We had no choice. We get our revenue from the state, right? And if we violate the state's mandate, I've got no way of justifying that."

COPS & DOUGHNUTS

But Chuck Rogalski, president of the Chamber of Commerce, fired back. He issued a press release saying the chamber objected to Governor Whitmer's mandates, and that if the city manager and mayor weren't willing to stick up for people's constitutional rights, he was.

"He wrote that if the attorney general of the state of Michigan is going to come after anybody and cite 'em for it, that he was more than willing to take the citation," Ryno explained.

After the chamber's disparaging press release, the city announced it was parting ways with the Chamber of Commerce. (As a note, Cops & Doughnuts is an active member of the chamber. Ken Hibl is a former trustee, and Ryno is a current trustee.)

"Chuck took a political stance and that's unfortunate. In the military, there are rules and people comply with those rules," said Ken Hibl, a former army colonel.

In the end, Chuck resigned—he had to because the chamber needs the city of Clare to function, Ryno said.

"He took a bullet for it and then the city re-engaged in everything. It was the only way we could mend it and get the connection back, and it worked out well," Ryno said.

The Summerfest went forward, and the city kept true to its word. For example, people were required to mask up and socially distance while waiting in line for free hot dogs, which were donated by Witbeck's Family Foods, Ken said.

"It was simple. No mask, no hot dog. They had a choice. And we kept people separated in the eating places, allowing family units to sit together," Ken said.

Ryno pointed out that Ken took part in Summerfest on his personal time, helping to grill the hot dogs. "I thought that was really good."

And despite the political dustup, all three men remain friends.

"We're all on good terms. I consider Chuck a friend," Ken said. "We were just on the other side of the political fence. We couldn't allow the event to be politicized, and that's what was happening when he said you're violating constitutional rights. I don't know what part of the Constitution Chuck was referring to, but he was certainly entitled to his own opinion."

Today, Bubba and Ryno are relieved to have the pandemic mostly behind them. The good news: the bakery never had to shut down and the business showed a robust bottom-line growth in both 2020 and 2021, when including the injection of PPP loans, which they didn't have to pay back.

Although a handful of bakery employees were infected with COVID, there were no deaths. He and Bubba (who did wear a mask, when required) never got COVID and chose to get vaccine and booster shots when they became available.

"I actually dug into the bakery history and what's kind of cool is we didn't lose anybody during COVID and we didn't lose anybody during the summer of 1918 either in the flu epidemic. I went back and I got the records from Clare County; there was thirty-nine people who died back during the summer of 1917, 1918, and none of them worked in the bakery. So the Clare City Bakery, which is now Cops & Doughnuts, survived every war, every flu, every virus, every depression, every recession. You know, it's made it through it all."

Chapter 16

COPS, DOUGHNUTS, AND A TEMPTING FUTURE

When the nine cops decided to buy Clare City Bakery back in 2009, they had a mission to revive their little town. The downtown was emptying out in the midst of a national recession leaving seven storefronts vacant; unemployment was stuck at 19 percent. People needed work.

For the cops, this was personal. They knew that more jobs would mean people would have enough money to pay their bills. They'd drink less, drug less, and commit fewer crimes of desperation.

The cops had faith that Clare would survive the recession and once again thrive. They weren't alone in their optimism, said historian Jon Ringelberg, author of *Clare County Murders: 1871 to 2020*.

"There was a downturn in the economy, but I don't think people in Clare ever felt like they'd become a

Real bromance matters.

wayside or a ghost town. They knew it would once again be a thriving town."

For one, Clare is uniquely located nearly smack dab in the middle of Michigan, where US 10 and US 27 intersect, making Clare the gateway to everywhere else. Back in the late 1800s, Clare was the state's transportation hub, with railroad cars delivering timber to Michigan sawmills in Saginaw and Muskegon. The town evolved into a farming community in the early 1900s, slowly grew, and rebounded in the 1980s when small machine shops opened, Jon said.

Now Clare is once again a transportation hub. Two trucking companies, which boast more than 200 trucks and tankers between them, deliver goods and plastic pellets around the state. Another large development is in the works with plans for scores of trucks to haul potash from a new plant in nearby Evart, according to Jon.

In the past thirteen years, the Cops & Doughnuts bakery has proved itself; the economy is once again booming and profits are solid and growing. Storefronts do go vacant but are quickly reoccupied. The downtown is a busy place!

Ryno and Bubba built bakery revenues to $3.4 million—far beyond what any of the nine cop owners could have dreamed of back in 2009. And they hope that someday new owners will take the bakery to the next level.

Looking at the big picture, the bakery opened in a recession, when jobs were hard to get. COVID sent unemployment soaring to a record high of 28.7 percent in April of 2020, but few people could or wanted to work in the midst of a pandemic. In March of 2022, unemployment dropped down to 7.5 percent. Although double the rate of the rest of the country (3.8 percent), the bakery

COPS & DOUGHNUTS

Ryno envisions enlarging doughnut distribution on the east side of the state.

and others are mightily struggling to fill positions. It's not unusual to arrive at a Clare restaurant only to find a closed sign along with an apology that there just isn't enough staff to operate.

Part of the reason is owed to the resurgence of manufacturing in Michigan, said Jim McBryde, CEO of the Middle Michigan Development Corporation.

"There were decades of offshoring, moving manufacturing into China, moving it to Mexico. Well, that trend has reversed," McBryde said. "When manufacturing came back to the United States, it came back disproportionately to Michigan. Manufacturing came back so fast that we're really struggling to connect the jobs with people right now. We just live in a population here where manufacturers are fighting over the same people."

The reality for retailers and restaurants—outfits like Cops & Doughnuts—is they can't offer the same wage and benefits packages as manufacturers do, he said.

But the good news is that profits are allowing the bakery to offer higher wages. Realistically, though, it's impossible to grow the bakery within the confines of Clare. If the bakery were to expand, Cops & Doughnuts would have to locate its next production hub in a different part of the state.

The other challenge is transitioning the bakery to new cop owners. Ryno and Bubba, both 59, aren't yet ready to retire, but when they do, they're planning on . . .

"World domination," Bubba said.

"The one thing I think we could do is to create a cartoon because little kids love us!" Ryno said.

"I would like to see this franchised, but I don't know how we'd ever do it," Bubba added.

Ryno envisions the new owners building a second production facility on the east side of the state someday. They could fan out distribution similar to the bicycle wheel model they use now, where goods are baked up in Clare and delivered to multiple locations within a two-and-a-half-hour radius.

But all this depends on finding perfect replacements for Bubba and Ryno: law-enforcement types with a passion for marketing and a willingness to work well beyond sixty hours a week.

"I always say, if you want to work forty–fifty hours a week, work for somebody else. Don't become an entrepreneur," Ryno said, laughing. "Whoever does get this, they've got to have a cop connection. Somehow we've got to keep that going because real cops, real bromance matters."

A SNAPSHOT OF THE NINE COP OWNERS

Brian "Dogman" Gregory is a career law enforcement officer. His career started in the early 1980s and continued until April 2022, when he retired as chief of the Clare Police Department. He and his wife, Denise, live in Harrison, Michigan. Brian is the father of three adult children and has four grandchildren. Brian "Dogman" trains dogs for law enforcement, his specialty for nearly three decades. He is an avid hunter and enjoys the outdoors. He says his law enforcement career is full of memories both good and bad, but wouldn't change it for the world.

Greg "Bulldog" Kolhoff was born and raised in central Michigan where he still lives today. He briefly left the area to serve his country in the U.S. Marine Corps. After returning home he pursued a career in law enforcement and firefighting and as an emergency services technician. He has been blessed to have been married over twenty years with three children and three grandchildren. Greg still serves his community as a police officer and firefighter.

Jeremy "Squirt" McGraw is a U.S. Army veteran and former officer of the Clare Police Department. He is married and has two children.

COPS & DOUGHNUTS

Dwayne "Midge" Miedzianowski gets his nickname from his challenging-to-spell last name and also the fact that he is the shortest of the nine cop owners. He joined the Clare City Police Reserves right out of high school, beginning his career in law enforcement.

His next job was as a juvenile probation officer for the Saginaw Chippewa Tribe in Mt. Pleasant, Michigan. From there he joined the tribal police department and went on to be the lieutenant in charge of the entire force.

In 2005, Midge became the chief of police for the Clare Police Department until 2011 when he became undersheriff for the Clare County Sheriff's Department in Harrison, Michigan.

John "Beaver" Pedjac was born in Clare, Michigan, and was raised on a small family farm south of town. After high school he decided to become a paramedic and an EMS instructor. John then joined the Clare Police Department in 1990. He has a passion for public service and has served his community in local elected government for many years. John has a beautiful, creative, and artful deaf daughter and a son who has grown into a man he's proud of!

Greg "Ryno" Rynearson was born and raised in Clare, Michigan. Ryno was drawn to the Clare Police Explorer Cadet program at age sixteen, inspired by his two older brothers, who served as auxiliary police officers with the Clare Police Department. Ryno had found his calling.

In 1982 he joined the Clare Police Auxiliary, and four years later, joined the Clare County Sheriff Department Reserves. In 1988 his paid police career began, first working with the sheriff's department until 1999 when he joined the Clare Police Department. He retired in 2013 to work full-time at the bakery—his second calling—and is often called a marketing genius. He serves as president of Cops & Doughnuts.

Ryno was married to Tammy for thirty-one years until her passing in February 2022, during the writing of this book. Ryno has three children and ten grandchildren.

Dave "Grasshopper" Saad began his law enforcement career with the Clare County Sheriff's Department. In 1999, he started his full-time career with the Clare City Police, where he now serves as chief. He is arguably the most serious of all the nine cop owners, his nickname owing to his quiet demeanor.

Rich "Junior" Ward gained his nickname given to him while bartending in college. He began his career at the Clare County Sheriff's Department and subsequently joined the Clare City Police Department. He also has worked for the Midland County Sheriff's Department in Midland, Michigan. He currently serves as the chief of police for the City of Coleman Police Department.

Rich is a fun-loving, upbeat guy who enjoys outdoor activities and going out with friends. He is also a childhood cancer survivor.

Alan "Bubba" White retired in 2013 after serving for thirty years in law enforcement, working both in Michigan and Alaska. A jovial, funny and imaginative sort, Bubba serves as vice president of Cops & Doughnuts.

Bubba has also been a landscape contractor, emergency

room specialist, paramedic, college instructor, chemical weapons trainer, school safety consultant, police reserve director, political candidate, and professional animal skinner.

He has authored four books, including *Alaska Behind Blue Eyes*, *Standing Ground*, *In Sheep's Clothing* and *Promise Not to Tell*. He is currently working on two more books. Bubba is also a professional speaker.

Bubba lives in the Clare area with his wife, Anete (Nettie), a Dutch Longhaar pointer named Esther, and an Australian Labradoodle named Mabel, whom Bubba fondly refers to as his "emergency back-up dog." They have two children.

Anne Stanton is the editorial director for Mission Point Press, a Traverse City, Michigan-based firm that provides a full slate of editorial, marketing and design services to independent authors. She has previously published *Publish to Win*, a marketing book aimed at independent authors.

She is a cofounder and interim director of the National Writers Series, which promotes youth literacy and hosts nationally renowned authors on the Traverse City Opera House stage. Anne previously worked as an award-winning reporter and as a researcher/editor for two *New York Times* bestselling books, *In Harm's Way* and *12 Strong*. Anne received a Master of Arts degree in journalism from the University of Michigan.

ACKNOWLEDGMENTS

The cop owners of Cops & Doughnuts received so much help with this project that it is nearly impossible to acknowledge all of the people involved.

First, we must thank our collaborative author, Anne Stanton, for somehow being able to work with the cop owners, interviewing local leaders and customers, and somehow putting it all together so it made sense. It must have been like herding cats. This book would not be possible without her drive, passion, and attention to detail. We would also like to thank the Mission Point Press team for making this book a reality and for all the outstanding resources they provided.

Others that were instrumental in this project include: Ken Hibl, Pat Humphrey, Travis Harrison, Sherry Kleinhardt, Jon Ringelberg, Lt. Josh Lator, Jim McBryde, Morgan Humphrey and Tim Cruttenden.

And finally, thank you to the citizens of Clare, Michigan, who have stood by this bunch of crazy cops that had a wild idea and saw it come together. This project would not be possible without their support.